Making Your Sales Team #1

Other books by Thomas L. Quick

The Ambitious Woman's Guide to a Successful Career (with Margaret
    V. Higginson)
How People Work Best
Increasing Your Sales Success
Inspiring People at Work
Manager's Guide to Lawful Termination
The Manager's Motivation Desk Book
Managing for Peak Performance
Managing People at Work Desk Guide
The Persuasive Manager
Quick Solutions
Unconventional Wisdom
Understanding People at Work

Making Your Sales Team #1

THOMAS L. QUICK

amacom

American Management Association

Library of Congress Cataloging-in-Publication Data

Quick, Thomas L.
    Making your sales team #1 / Thomas L. Quick.
        p.   cm.
    Includes bibliographical references.
    ISBN 0-8144-7741-0
        *1. Selling—Personnel management. 2. Sales personnel—Training
of. 3. Employee motivation. I. Title. II. Title: Making your
sales team number 1.*
    HF5439.5.Q53   1992
    658.8'1—dc20   *91-30475*
                                                                    CIP

Printing number

10   9   8   7   6   5   4   3   2   1

To
Lauren, Amanda, and Kelcy

Contents

Introduction

It is hard to imagine a responsibility more demanding than managing salespeople in the field. For one thing, control is much more complicated when you must manage from a distance. For another, many of your salespeople are likely to be highly competitive and value their autonomy. Your stars, especially, may resist what they consider to be close supervision on your part. Then there is you. If you are a typical field manager, you've come up through sales yourself. You can't be faulted for believing that your sales approach is the best. Ironically, the very qualities that made you successful as a salesperson—your competitiveness, your aloneness, your confidence in your style of selling—tend to work against you in managing others.

You can turn that competitiveness, however, into a drive to make your sales team the company's number-one team. You learned how to make yourself a winner. Now you can help *all* your salespeople be stars. There is no reason to have a multitiered sales force, with the stars at the top, the strugglers and stragglers at the bottom, and the fair and borderline producers in a large gray area in between. The only way to run a sales force in these days of intense competition from companies here and abroad is for you, as manager, to have the clear and continuing intention to push, pull, and persuade your salespeople to aim for the top—to be the very best they can.

Upgrading the effectiveness of your salespeople will indeed be a continuing effort on your part, because we are never as effective in every situation as we would like to be. Sharpening selling skills is an ongoing process, because the world will always be a little different tomorrow. The business environment never remains static. There will be new competitors or revitalized old ones. The people who make the buying decisions will move on, out, or up, making way for new decision makers. The economy will present opportunities or challenges as we experience inflation or recession, downturns or upturns, war or peace, bear markets or bull markets. Nothing, we have learned, is so constant as change.

Success won't be achieved by selling the same way and at the same skill level day after day, month after month, year after year. And you won't become an effective manager by simply maintaining the present level of performance in your sales force. You need only look around you to see the disappearances of companies and managements that tried to perpetuate the past. There's really no such thing as maintenance management. You either go forward or fall back.

The key to a continual upgrading of the effectiveness of your salespeople is training. We often make the mistake of viewing training as something that is done in a classroom in order to fix something that is wrong. The reality is that real learning—new knowledge or skills or techniques—takes place after the classroom work has been completed. Learning in adults requires application and feedback. You can drill and role-play and lecture all you want in a classroom, but real learning occurs after the salespeople return to the field, apply what they have been taught in the training program, and get feedback on how well they put the content into practice. There's nothing wrong with rehearsing closing techniques in the training program and receiving the applause and approval of the trainer and other trainees, but the real test comes with prospects. If the salesperson closes the sale, that is the most powerful and valuable feedback.

You are a critical factor in the training of your salespeople. You provide them with opportunities to practice what the trainers have preached. You supervise their experimentation with new knowledge or skills and give feedback that supplements and refines what they receive during sales interviews. Probably most important, you provide positive reinforcement and other rewards.

Thus, lasting improvements in sales performance are taken out of the classroom and into the territory, if you take control of that learning. As your salespeople become more effective and more skilled, you'll be amply rewarded with higher productivity, a more enthusiastic sales force, the esteem of the home office and other field managers, perhaps more money, and certainly more pleasure and gratification.

How receptive will your salespeople be to your efforts to help them perform better? You can expect most of them to be very turned on. As I discuss later in this book, growth is a major motivator. People respond powerfully to the possibility that they will be more knowledgeable, skilled, competent, and experienced in the months ahead than they are now. When you are the provider of opportunities and help that will result in such growth, you can expect a loyal, committed, highly motivated sales force.

This book advocates that you take a total team approach, that you devote yourself to raising the performance level of everyone in your group from the stars at the top to the strugglers at the bottom. Of course, this requires different techniques. In fact, the practice of management should be a one-to-one proposition. Managers who overlook this fact don't get the response they want from their salespeople. This book tells you how to deal with your stars to help them produce even more spectacularly. You'll find many recommendations for helping your middle-level salespeople move closer to the top. And you'll receive guidelines for dealing with those who are floundering at the bottom.

Chapter 1 describes what it takes to build a top-producing team. Many field managers actually create impediments for themselves in upgrading the effectiveness of their salespeople. You'll have a chance to check yourself against some of these barriers to make sure you aren't inadvertently getting in your own way. It's also important for you to understand what motivates people at work. You do not, strictly speaking, motivate anyone but yourself. But you can identify the motivating forces in your salespeople and harness them for their and your benefit. Chapter 1 also discusses the special learning needs of adults. The four R's for the effective training and development of your people will help you retain this essential knowledge.

No matter how much you value action plans for improved competence, they won't be very effective if the salespeople don't buy into them. Chapter 2, therefore, concentrates on how you can enlist them in the continuing change effort. You'll usually be successful if you employ the same selling skills that made you successful as a salesperson. You may have to do some persuading and negotiating, but those are skills in which you've had plenty of experience. Your prospects didn't buy from you unless you could show them that the benefits you offered met their wants and needs. Neither will many of your salespeople.

Chapter 3 emphasizes your role as a partner in the change effort. This is a reality that some managers overlook. They seem to favor the idea of winding their salespeople up and leaving them to do it all alone. There are many partnership roles you can play—mentor, coach, hand-holder, resource, teacher, guide, rewarder, and don't forget listener. Sometimes that's the most helpful partner you can be: someone to listen patiently and nonjudgmentally.

Chapter 4 advises you on how you can give criticism that motivates. Most managers seem to have a genuine problem with criticizing because they fear that negative feedback demotivates and demoralizes. But when criticism is given according to the guidelines in Chapter 4, it can have a potent motivational value. Salespeople, far from being depressed or resentful, find the feedback helpful in getting the kinds of results they want. No one really likes to make mistakes or create barriers to effectiveness, so you'll often find that your corrective criticism is welcome. But when your corrective feedback doesn't work, you have to consider that your floundering salesperson is miscast. First, however, you owe it to yourself, the salesperson in trouble, and the company to make a last reasonable attempt to save the poor performer. Chapter 4 also guides you through the counseling process, the action improvement plan, and, if everything fails, how to apply whatever sanctions you've decided on: termination, transfer, or demotion.

Finally, Chapter 5 shows you how you can ensure that the improvement in your salespeople's effectiveness is made permanent through the rewards you can bestow. Many managers, whether they work inside or outside in the field, have a restricted notion of the power of rewards. Chapter 5 helps you expand your thinking about positive reinforcement and rewards that make the work more valuable to your salespeople.

The specific recommendations in this book for improving the performance of your sales team are based on research findings that have been developed over the past sixty years. Managing is often mistakenly termed a "soft" science, perhaps even more art than science. Nothing is further from the truth. Thanks to the research in the behavioral sciences in the United States since the early 1930s, we know what makes people want to commit themselves to the objectives of their companies and management. And drawing from the extensive work in adult education in the past few decades, we have a good understanding of how people learn, change, and improve their effectiveness. All of these concepts, theories, and conclusions represent powerful tools for you in helping your salespeople get more of the results they—and you—want.

Once a very insightful man told me that managing is a function of training. It was a revolutionary perspective. I had always heard it the other way around—that training was a function of managing—but I came to understand what he meant. Your primary obligation is to develop the most effective work group that you can. But that developing never stops, for at least two reasons. The first is that your people need to grow. Growth is necessary for their job satisfaction, well-being, and motivation. Simply continuing to do essentially the same thing is not enough to encourage them to sustain their commitment to the work. The second reason that development must be ongoing is, as I have already pointed out, that the conditions under which you and your salespeople do business are constantly changing, presenting all of you with new problems and challenges.

No successful businessperson remains so by standing still. In the decade ahead, you will face fiercer demands than any manager has ever encountered. In virtually every industry, economists predict that there will be much shaking out. In previous decades, businesspeople could say, with justification, "We make money whatever we do." But that complacency is exceedingly dangerous now. Our economy has gone global. Somewhere in the world, most of us who sell can expect to find someone who is prepared to try to outproduce us—in both quantity and quality—underprice us, and outmanage us.

The key to prosperity, perhaps even survival, is better managing and better training. For the manager who supervises salespeople in the field, the two functions are the same.

Making Your Sales Team #1

KEY TO CHAPTER 1

When salespeople commit themselves to any change for the better—to become more effective at what they do or to get more positive results more often—they do so because they see how important the rewards are to them personally. Any change they see as valuable and rewarding becomes a potential motivating force. As a manager, you too are motivated by drives, goals, and desires. But you must always bear in mind that what is important to you is not necessarily important to your salespeople. They may not respond to the same forces you do.

Contemporary managers deal with a diversity of personalities, motivations, and satisfactions. To be effective with your salespeople, you must know and understand what drives them. And before you can help them better their skills and competence, you need to grasp the realities of how adults learn new skills and acquire new knowledge. Of course, these facts about managing people were always true; it's just that managers of the past didn't fully appreciate them. Chances are that you, with your more sophisticated understanding, can get better results than your predecessors.

Unfortunately, many of the traditional managerial practices in sales management are still around. Field managers continue to create their own barriers to success. This chapter reviews some of the management functions that work and some that don't. You'll have no problem identifying which is which.

Following is a checklist of field sales management effectiveness. It provides you with an overview of what this book is all about and allows you to assess your current practices and see where you may be able to increase the impact you have on your salespeople.

Checklist of Field Sales Management Effectiveness

Following are a number of statements that refer to key areas in field sales management. How many of them *generally* correspond with your practice and beliefs?

	Yes	No
1. I periodically and regularly set performance goals with all of my salespeople.		✓

	Yes	No

2. I firmly believe that at least most of my salespeople want to do a better job, no matter how successful they are now. _____ _____

3. I have a good idea of the personal goals that each of my salespeople hopes to achieve through selling. _____ _____

4. When visiting salespeople, I usually look for ways to help them become even more effective. _____ _____

5. When I see skillful performance by my salespeople, I make it a point to comment on it as specifically as I can so they will know what to continue doing. _____ _____

6. I never assume that my salespeople know what I admire about their performance; I tell them frequently and specifically. _____ _____

7. I try to spend as much time individually with my stars as I do with my poor performers. _____ _____

8. I periodically and regularly communicate to all my salespeople what I expect from them in terms of performance standards and goals. _____ _____

9. When I see performance that I can praise or that I should correct, I give feedback as quickly and as specifically as possible. _____ _____

10. My salespeople are seldom surprised by my formal evaluations or appraisals of their performance because I have given them feedback throughout the year. _____ _____

11. I make sure that I communicate regularly with all of my salespeople, from top to bottom in production. _____ _____

12. When I see that a salesperson's productivity is below my standards, I take corrective action. If the action doesn't work, I schedule a formal counseling session with the person. _____ _____

13. I never conclude a counseling session without getting the salesperson's agreement on a specific action plan for improvement—

Yes   No

unless, of course, the reasons for the person's poor performance are determined to be external factors beyond his or her control. _____ _____

14. When a salesperson leaves a counseling session, he or she knows what sanctions I intend to apply if the action plan is not followed. He or she further knows that I will apply them as I have announced. _____ _____

15. When I must give negative feedback or criticism to a salesperson, I make sure that I talk only about his or her behavior. I do not refer to the person's personality, attitudes, or motives. I stick with what I can observe. _____ _____

16. When I suggest a possible improvement to a salesperson, I take into consideration whether it will suit that person's selling style and strengths. _____ _____

17. When I measure a person's performance, I do so in terms of my standards, goals, and expectations rather than comparing it with the performance of other salespeople in the group. _____ _____

18. When working with my star performers, I make sure that I always have some suggestions for their improved effectiveness, no matter how small the improvements might be. _____ _____

19. I make sure that all of my salespeople understand that rewards and perks are based on performance, not on factors that have little or nothing to do with their productivity. _____ _____

20. I present my training and coaching as a sign of how I value a salesperson rather than as a message that the person needs to fix his or her performance in some manner. _____ _____

Analysis

The twenty statements you've just responded to deal with your perceptions and management style in working with your salespeople. You'll note that I asked you to respond to the statements based on your *general* practice. There is no significant scoring. If you responded no, that you do not follow the practice or have the perception described in a statement, then this is certainly an area you'll want to think about further. If you responded yes to all the statements, you are entitled to regard yourself as an exceptionally enlightened manager of salespeople.

All of the statements will be amplified in the chapters that follow. I'm confident that whether you seek to fill a gap in your management or you want to refine or fine-tune what you already do to some extent, you'll find useful recommendations in this book.

1

What It Takes to Build a Top-Producing Team

"Every day, in every way, I am getting better and better." During the 1920s, in one of America's recurring preoccupations with self-improvement and self-healing, these words by the Frenchman Emile Coué were quoted frequently. Then, in the 1980s, inspired by consultant and author Tom Peters, we were urged to excellence. Now, in the 1990s, we're all out to win the Malcolm Baldrige award for Total Quality Management.

Throughout the decades, Americans have exhibited a passion for the total, the ultimate, the all-out. But I remember some more reasonable words about excellence from an executive a few years back: "I think excellence is a fine goal," he said, "but meantime, I'll just be happy with steady improvement, even if it is sometimes small." This book is all about steady improvement and the will to win. Your salespeople want to become more skilled, more competent, more effective in their selling. And you, as their manager, would like to see them be a winning sales team, perhaps number one in the company. But the reality is that most of us don't transform ourselves in great leaps and bounds. Coué was only half right: We can get better and better every day, but not in every way. We don't change on a broad front; we improve a sector at a time.

Helping Your Salespeople Grow

First, your salespeople must have the will to become more effective, to grow, to change. Undoubtedly, you've already discovered that they have that will, since it's built in to most people. Your salespeople have a natural desire to be more effective at what they do next month and next year than they are this month and this year. The eminent social scientist Frederick Herzberg, in research that became famous in the 1960s and 1970s, established that the vast majority of people at work are motivated by achievement, more responsibility, advancement, and the possibility for growth.

But they must also have the opportunity to grow in competence and knowledge. Your contribution, probably the most important one you can make to their success, is to provide them with that opportunity. If you do, your rewards will be much the same as theirs: satisfaction, a sense of achievement, excitement, perhaps even more fun in your work. In addition, you all might make considerably more money. And there'll be a lot of glory to go around as you push your people to be the best they can be. In the process, you'll be building monuments to yourself: your successful salespeople. There's nothing wrong with that—far from it. That's what good managers do. They achieve their goals by helping their subordinates reach theirs.

Knowing the Goals That Turn Them On

In the three decades that I have worked with managers to help them become more effective, I've been mystified by the reluctance or even resistance of some to learn anything about what their subordinates hope to achieve for themselves through their work. I suspect that those who wish to remain in the dark really don't want to know very much about their people. Or else they don't know how to talk with their subordinates—and they would probably be poor listeners anyway. Certainly some managers haven't established the necessary trust and credibility in their relationships with their employees that would encourage those employees to speak openly about what they want from their efforts.

All human activities are directed toward the achievement of goals. We don't act unless we have a goal toward which to move. Furthermore, these goals must be valuable to us, or we wouldn't bother trying to reach them. The lesson for managers is simple: If you want your folks to help you achieve your goals, show them that in doing so they will achieve something valuable for themselves. As with any sales prospect you had as a salesperson, you must make an effort to know what that something valuable is. Only then can you be sure that the benefit you hold out meets their needs and wants. Managers who walk around not knowing play management roulette. Sometimes they win, but the odds are against them.

Managing Motivation

Many managers today know very little about the motivation of their people because those of us who are supposed to enlighten them don't. My experience in training, however, leads me to believe that most trainers don't know much about what motivates people either. I frequently hear managers ask, "How can I motivate my people?" You can't. You can motivate yourself, but motivation is not something you can do to someone else. The "doing to" school has been adequately described by Frederick Herzberg as the KITA (the kick in the behind) approach to managing. Managers who follow this school of thought find that they have to keep kicking.

Then there is the question, "What do I do with an unmotivated salesperson?" The answer is that you bury him because he must be dead; there is no such thing as an unmotivated person. What managers who ask such a question are really saying is that their people don't seem to be motivated to do what they, the managers, want them to do—a situation I'll deal with shortly.

Motivation comes from within. Each of us has our own motivating forces. Unfortunately, that means that if twenty people report to you, there will probably be twenty sets of motivators. Can you manage the motivation of your salespeople? Of course you can. When you find out what turns a particular salesperson on, you can provide every opportunity for that person to obtain what is valuable to him or her: achievement, self-esteem, recognition, professional growth, status, power, wealth, or glory, to name just a few.

Using Expectancy Theory

There's nothing mysterious about motivating people at work. There's a dandy theory to help you construct an entire system of management called expectancy theory. It's simple, it's practical, it's mainstream psychology, and it works. Best of all, most of your management colleagues have probably not heard of it, so right off you have a competitive edge. Here, in its simplicity and completeness, is expectancy theory:

> *Human behavior is a function of (a) the value of the reward that people see will result from an action, choice, or decision they select; and (b) their expectation that they will be able to achieve that reward without undue risk or effort [this is the expectancy of the theory].*

If you apply expectancy theory to all of your dealings with your subordinates, your success ratio in persuading them to do what you want them to do will increase enormously. Because, as you can see, you are really persuading them to do what is valuable to them.

The formula is simple. Make sure that your salespeople see the changes you propose as valuable to them. Is it worth their while to make them? At the same time, help them realize that they can enjoy the rewards the new behaviors will bring. You, as manager, can increase their self-confidence and help them believe that they will be successful. In short, make the change:

- Interesting to them
- Valuable to them
- Easy for them

You've always done that with prospects. That's why you were a successful salesperson. You persuaded your prospects that what you had to offer was valuable and rewarding to them. Then you made it as easy as possible for them to buy from you.

Expectancy theory touches on every choice we make in every aspect of our lives. You'll find the concept useful in every managerial act you perform, in every contact you have with your salespeople. You'll find its universality in the choices you make: from the tasks you choose to start your day to the order of the field visits you make—will the return on your time be greater in Indianapolis than in Dayton?—from the car you buy for the family to what you order for lunch. You make choices that promise the most value for you. However, if you believe that your initial choice will involve too much effort or risk—if it's a long shot—you may switch to an option that has less value but greater attainability. For example, take your vacation plans. You want to go to Czechoslovakia, but you've been told that the availability of good accommodations is very limited, and what you get may not be what you want. The attainability of the enjoyment—the reward—has been reduced. You may settle for a visit to Switzerland, where you know that what you want will be readily available.

Take your career. Perhaps there was a time when you dreamed of aiming for the CEO position. But now, as you grow older and take more pleasure in your family, you decide that your original ambition is less desirable. You just don't want to put in the extra hours that would mark you as a potential CEO candidate. So you scale down your choice to a less demanding position.

In the same way, your salespeople place different values on what they do. Not everyone on your sales force wants to become wealthy or become part of management or become number one in the group. This is a reality that you must recognize when you work to persuade them to become more productive. In Chapter 2, I talk more about how you can be effective in persuading them to improve, to buy into your performance goals.

How Adults Learn

A teacher once told me how to expand my vocabulary. "It isn't enough," she said, "to look the word up in the dictionary. You must use it. Speak and write sentences using the word correctly. Then it will become yours." Absolutely correct. That's how we learn: through application. Employees in companies are often trained in classrooms and meetings—that is, the content of the training program is presented there. There may even be some role-playing and exercises. But the most effective learning takes place under real-life conditions, back on the job. The most effective feedback your salespeople can receive occurs when the new knowledge or technique is applied, and either it works or it doesn't.

For example, your salespeople can be drilled in various closing techniques. But using those closing techniques with prospects is how they actually learn and retain. Either they succeed or they don't. The problem is that when they don't get an order, they sometimes don't know why. That's where you come in. You're there to observe what they do in closing that might impede their effectiveness. They might use words that don't quite invite commitment, such as, "Does this make sense to you?" Or they might talk past the point of asking for action, thereby blunting the impact of the close. Or they might break the silence after asking the prospect to go along, giving the prospect an "out" or release from the pressure.

They need to apply what they've heard in the classroom. They need feedback on how well they've applied it. And when they have done it well, they need to have their success reinforced with some kind of recognition or reward.

Getting the New Behavior You Want

Every time you talk with a salesperson, you have an opportunity to shape his or her behavior for the better. These days you hear the terms *behavior modification* and *behavior conditioning*. Neither is synonymous with manipulation or brainwashing. The principles of behavior conditioning were developed in laboratories using pigeons and rodents. For example, a pigeon would be taught to press a lever to get a food pellet; that was its reward for pressing the lever. As long as each press of the lever produced a pellet, the pigeon would continue to do so. Its behavior was being positively reinforced. When the food was withdrawn, the pigeon's lever-pressing behavior was negatively reinforced and it would eventually stop pressing the lever. The pigeon's behavior was shaped by the rewards or the absence of them.

Managers have the same tool in the workplace. When you want to see a type of behavior repeated, you reward or reinforce it. When you want to "extinguish" the behavior, you stop rewarding it or you punish it, which is a bit extreme. In managing the motivation of people and in shaping the new behavior you want, you should follow these five steps built on expectancy theory.

1. *Tell salespeople what you expect them to do.* Periodically sit down with them and set forth the goals you would like them to achieve and the standards at which you expect them to perform. A goal might be an annual volume of at least $300,000 per person. A standard could be a minimum number of twenty calls each week on prospects. You can also do this for performance improvement. You might change certain goals for a salesperson, for example, from an average of twenty calls a week to twenty-three.

2. *Make the work valuable.* "What's in it for me?" the salesperson asks when you suggest a change in the way he or she sells. The answer might be more money, a chance for promotion, more glory, greater esteem, higher status, and so on. Just as you always did with prospects when you were in the field, you have to understand your salespeople's needs and wants in order to influence them.

3. *Make the work doable.* You can train, coach, guide, be a partner, suggest, be a role model, and encourage. There are any number of ways in which you can make success appear more attainable.

4. *Give feedback.* Your salespeople need to know how they're doing. If they're doing it right, they want reinforcement. If they're not, they want corrective help.

5. *Reward successful behavior.* When they get it right, they appreciate praise and other reinforcement from you, so they know what behavior to repeat.

If you follow these five steps in managing your people and helping them improve their performance, you'll see significant and profitable results. This kind of managing is open and honest. There are no hidden agendas, no manipulation.

The New Sophistication in Sales Management

Selling has changed enormously since I began my career as a salesman in the early 1950s. Unfortunately, managers' knowledge of what motivates people at work has not kept up. In 1954, many sales managers simply assumed that everyone entering the sales force had essentially the same motivation: to make money. In fact, it was generally assumed that most of us entered corporate life to achieve similar rewards and to attain the American dream—a house of our own, one or two cars in the garage, an annual vacation, perhaps a membership in the country club, and the wherewithal to send our children to college.

Salespeople were different in that everyone knew we wanted to make money. Why else would someone choose a risky, confidence-bashing line of work? After five years in the field, I shocked my bosses by announcing that I was ready for a change. None of the other field group insurance specialists seemed to be unhappy doing the same thing year after year and earning a higher and higher income. We weren't expected to become bored. This view persisted for many years. As late as the middle 1970s, I was asked by a sales manager what he should do about a former high producer who had reached a plateau and showed no great desire to come off. When I learned that the salesman had been doing essentially the same thing for fifteen years, the reason was obvious. How many people can tolerate doing the same thing year after year?

We now understand that people are motivated to grow, that they usually respond favorably to challenge and change. The pervasive belief that people resist change is a myth. People resist when they feel threatened, and with good reason. But if change represents an opportunity to grow, to become more skilled, to actualize oneself, it is generally welcomed. But thirty years ago, few people recognized how important it is to most of us to become more skilled, more knowledgeable, more competent, and more capable.

There was also a prevailing belief in the so-called sales personality. The stereotype of a salesman—and it was mostly men in those days—was a person who was extroverted, thick-skinned, not terribly sensitive or introspective, certainly not intellectual. They were doers rather than thinkers. And they were said to "like people," whatever that meant. One of my early managers told a marvelous story about that cliché: He was recruiting for a sales position that he had advertised in the local newspaper. One by one the applicants came to his office for an interview. Time after time he would ask, "Why do you want to sell?" And the answer, almost invariably, was, "Because I like people." It became a joke. Finally, when one applicant gave the standard answer, the manager looked quizzical and said, "You do?" It threw the candidate off stride. After a moment of confusion, the young man asked, "Don't you?" "Only if they buy from me," the manager replied.

In the past, there was an adversarial flavor to the sales transaction. One sales trainer at a point early in my career referred to prospects as pigeons. The sales interview was often seen as a contest, in which the salesperson had to be shrewder and faster on his feet than the prospect.

Much sales training in those days was actually product knowledge. In group insurance sales in my company, it was assumed that the fellow with the sharper pencil got the business. I don't recall having a training session in which we were drilled in closing techniques, for example. Although I was reasonably successful in the field, I'm sure I lost a fair amount of business because I operated on the assumption that if I was smarter than my competitors, knew more about the business than they did, and had competitive rates, I would get the business.

The hiring of salespeople was based on some kind of profile of the "sales personality." Recruiters also looked for certain kinds of people that would fit in with the culture of the company. The phrase, "He's our kind of guy," was heard frequently. Many organizations tried to achieve a monochromatic appearance. When my boss sat in my office and exclaimed, "You're not like the other salesmen," I accepted the reality that my days with the company were numbered.

We now realize that selling is a much more complex issue. Relying too heavily on product knowledge can be self-defeating. Buying decisions are made on several levels—the rational, the emotional, the psychological. Furthermore, the sales interview is more properly a transaction, a negotiation, a giving and taking.

The successful salesperson must be sensitive to the prospect's needs, wants, and perceptions. It's not a matter of, "Here's my superior product," but rather, "Here's how my superior product will meet your needs and benefit you."

We also see that managing salespeople in the field is more complicated. We don't look for sales personalities as such. Some of the very best salespeople I know defy the stereotype. They can be thinkers, sensitive, even introspective. We recognize that many types of personalities can engage successfully in selling, and that their motivating factors can be quite diverse. Managers who do not accept this reality of diverse motivations are going to hamper their effectiveness in managing their salespeople to excellence.

Avoiding Barriers to Your Effectiveness

Inadequate understanding of what motivates people to do a better job is only one self-imposed barrier that prevents field managers from being effective in helping salespeople increase their productivity. Here are some common managerial practices that can get in your way:

• *Concentrating unduly on the squeaky wheels.* Salespeople who flounder and fail and cry for help unceasingly can drain your time and energy. Some managers hate to give up trying to turn these people around because they don't want to admit failure. Good advice is to know when to cut your losses and run. Set a limit on your salvage efforts; when you are satisfied that you have provided the sinking salesperson with every reasonable kind of help but still have not seen the results you want and are entitled to, cut the person loose. You'll probably be doing both of you a favor. Just as some managers hate to give up on the failures, some failures hate to admit that they are indeed in the wrong line of work.

• *Neglecting star performers.* People who produce well can get awfully lonely out there. Their managers spend most of their time with the squeaky wheels, or they have some misguided belief that the star wants to be left alone. I've known some field managers who were actually intimidated by their high producers. Your stars generally want your attention, even though they may also seek as much autonomy as possible. They want recognition of their success and superior skills. They also want to increase their competence. They look to you for that. Dealing with the star is different from working with the lesser performer, but don't succumb to the myth that your star doesn't need you.

• *Not clearly communicating the goals and standards you expect of your people.* Because you are busy, you may forget to have that periodic talk with each salesperson about what is expected during the coming year. Or else you assume that the salespeople know what is expected of them. In either case, there's much room for misunderstanding. Salespeople perform in the way they believe the manager wants, which can easily be misinterpreted. Keep your salespeople feeling that they are truly members of the team. Schedule at least one individual discussion of general goals and standards with each salesperson each year. Don't let them get too far away from you.

• *Giving feedback that demoralizes and demotivates.* Many managers find it painful and embarrassing to criticize the performance of their salespeople when they fail to work up to ability, make serious errors, or experience other kinds of performance deficiencies. But people need feedback if they are to do a good job. They accept that fact, even if it is unpleasant to hear that they are not doing something right or well. Some managers will go to great lengths to avoid criticizing their salespeople. They may give ambiguous or confusing feedback rather than addressing the problem head-on. Or they let the frustration, disappointment, and anger over a salesperson's mistakes build to the boiling point and then let hurtful criticisms spill over. Other managers allow themselves to be swept into talking about personality, attitudes, and motives, which are easy to misinterpret, rather than sticking to actual behavior. The result is an aggrieved salesperson who finds it difficult to work through his or her resentment to make the desired improvements.

• *Failing to recognize achievement and improvement.* When you ask for improved performance and get it, be sure to acknowledge it. Otherwise a salesperson may think you don't really care or that you are taking him or her for granted. Reinforcing changed and improved behavior is the way you can encourage its repetition. Failing to recognize improved behavior will result in the salesperson eventually discontinuing it.

• *Trying to impose unsuitable selling techniques and styles, ignoring an individual's strengths and idiosyncrasies.* Don't say, "Hey, you ought to try Carl's closing techniques." Or, "Here's a good way to handle objections that Jane has used. You should try it too." At one point in my career, I was told that I had to use a canned presentation verbatim. The words, the writing style, the organization were foreign to me, and I was not successful using it. Comparing selling styles or freely borrowing techniques from other salespeople may not be helpful. Your salespeople have varying strengths. Go with the grain. Adapt techniques and advice to a salesperson's unique way of operating.

• *Not having a systematic plan for development of salespeople.* A hit-or-miss approach to upgrading salespeople's effectiveness usually doesn't work and may backfire if salespeople become cynical and don't take you seriously. Or you might be trying to attempt too much at one time in periodic campaigns for improvement. The best approach is steady and ongoing, taking small steps. People usually don't improve on a broad front or during a frantic campaign.

Training Up and Out

One issue that many managers don't want to confront is the danger of improving a salesperson's competence to the point where they lose him or her. If a salesperson has ambition to get ahead, there's not much you can do to keep that person "down on the farm." But get as much from that person as you can while you can. Your help in making that salesperson more valuable both personally and in the marketplace can contribute to increased motivation. Trying to dampen ambition is futile. It's a tool for you, so use it.

When I sold sales training programs for a certain company, I was restless and dissatisfied because I wanted to join the staff that wrote the programs for salespeople. However, my managers kept putting me off when I tried to talk about eventually making the switch from the field to inside. They didn't want to lose me, and they discouraged me from even thinking about leaving the field. I did anyway. Regrettably, there was unnecessary bitterness on both sides. It's unwise to risk building frustration, resentment, or bitterness. That ambitious salesperson may someday be in a position to create trouble for you, or much goodwill. In the more immediate future, your discouraged salesperson may go from a high level of productivity to a much lower one.

A more sensible approach is to suggest a contract when you see that your restless salesperson is determined to move on. For example, you might say, "If you continue to work as hard as you have for the time you remain with me, I'll help you get the credentials and knowledge you need to reach your goal. And I'll give you the very best recommendation I can when you're ready to make your move." Such a contract gives you a better chance to have a high producer right up to the end, rather than an uncommitted, possibly mediocre salesperson. You'll also make a lasting, grateful friend who may someday return the favor.

The Four R's

To help you remember and utilize the realities of motivation and adult learning in your field training of salespeople, I offer the following simple formula, employing the four R's:

1. *Relevance* of the improvement to a salesperson. It isn't enough to say, "Here's what you should do, because I, as manager, believe you should." Adults tend to learn only what they regard as useful and valuable to them. So you must make the change relevant to the salesperson.
2. *Realistic* application of the new knowledge. Real learning usually doesn't take place in a classroom or by talking about it. The new skill has to be applied and practiced under real-life conditions. If it isn't, it will probably be lost and forgotten. The retention curve after training is your worst enemy. About 90 percent of what was taught in the

classroom or the meeting will be gone within three months unless it has been applied and reinforced.

3. *Resources* the manager has to offer. You can help a salesperson set learning goals that are attainable without undue effort and risk. You can work with him or her as a partner in that change. You can coach, train, suggest, guide, and give feedback.

4. *Rewards* for successful change and improvement. You can make the change worthwhile and positively reinforce the new behavior so that it is likely to be continued.

Training salespeople in the field is solidly rooted in these four R's. *Relevance,* of course, is another term for importance and value. People choose to do what is valuable to them. Expectancy theory explains that. And in Chapter 2, you'll see how you can increase the value of learning to a salesperson. The *realistic* application of the new knowledge and the *resources* you offer form the basis for the discussion of your role as partner in the change in Chapter 3. You can make the learning more doable (expectancy theory again). Finally, you can make sure that a salesperson feels *rewarded* for having made a successful change, both through the person's own internal rewards, dealt with in Chapter 2, and through the external rewards you have at your disposal, as discussed in Chapter 5.

In summary, when you want to change your salespeople's performance and push them toward greater competence and higher productivity, use what you know about the motivation and learning of people at work, and remember to make the change:

- Interesting to them
- Valuable to them
- Easy for them

No one in the company has a better opportunity than you for helping and guiding your people to be a winning sales team—for themselves and for you.

KEY TO CHAPTER 2

While Chapter 1 was primarily concerned with *why* people buy, this chapter offers advice on *how* they buy. Your experience has undoubtedly shown you that it isn't enough for you to see value in change or in some new improvement goal. Your salespeople must agree with that perception of value. Some managers simply try to will their subordinates to agree with them, but that usually has very limited impact. For an enduring impact, you'll probably have to resort to your influencing skills: You'll work to understand their drives; you'll invite them to help you set goals for improvement; you'll encourage them to enjoy their feelings of achievement, satisfaction, and growth in their successful efforts to upgrade their effectiveness.

Following is a self-assessment checklist that will help you measure just how successful you have been in bringing about changed behavior in your salespeople. Answer the questions as candidly as you can. Your answers will set the stage for Chapter 2.

Assessing Your Success in Bringing About Change

How would you rate yourself in your ability to recognize the need for change and improvement in your salespeople and your success in helping them achieve those goals? Some of the reasons that you are—or are not—successful are contained in the following questions:

	Yes	No
1. Do you believe that most of your salespeople will follow your suggestions for improved performance once you carefully explain how they can achieve such improvement?	_____	_____
2. Do you sometimes wonder why a salesperson fails to act on your suggestion after you have explained the what and how of the suggestion in detail?	_____	_____
3. Do you worry that some of your salespeople quickly forget your counsel and suggestions after you've left their territories?	_____	_____

	Yes	No
4. Do you suspect that some of your salespeople pay lip service to your advice?	———	———
5. Do you become frustrated when you return to a salesperson's territory to find that he or she is not following your suggestions correctly?	———	———
6. Do you on occasion become irritated because a salesperson seems to believe that he or she knows better than you what changes in technique are right?	———	———
7. Do you ever experience "yes, butting" from salespeople when you try to explain how they could improve their selling by incorporating your suggestions?	———	———
8. Do you sometimes get upset when you see a gap between a salesperson's assurance that he or she will adopt your advice and what actually happens in the performance?	———	———
9. Do you get annoyed when a salesperson resists your advice to adopt successful techniques employed by other salespeople in your region?	———	———
10. Do you sometimes hear what you believe are rationalizations from your salespeople about why your suggestions didn't work after all?	———	———

Analysis

If you answered yes to one or more of the questions, take some comfort in the fact that many of the behaviors described are quite common, even in sales forces that are generally effective and productive. There may be multiple reasons for the irritating, bewildering, or frustrating behaviors. All of them are dealt with in the chapters that follow, but there are certain generic roots:

• You may not be applying to your salespeople the same techniques you have used successfully in the past to persuade your prospects to buy from you. People often resist ideas, suggestions, and advice from others—even their managers—when they don't believe that the proposed changes are going to pay off for them. Those changes may have been suitable and profitable for others, but if salespeople don't see the proposed changes as meeting their wants and needs and being rewarding to them in terms of higher productivity, they'll resist. When you encountered this resistance in prospects, you realized that more selling was indicated. You also recognized the probability that you hadn't involved the prospect sufficiently: linking what you have to offer to what he or she wants. In short, your benefits have to meet the prospect's needs.

• Application and practice of any new skill or technique are usually necessary if the learning is to be complete and permanent. You can explain and demonstrate all you wish, but it's a salesperson's ability to translate your ideas into personal success that matters. Therefore, don't leave the salesperson with simply the idea and the explanation. Satisfy yourself and the salesperson that the practice represents the preaching.

• Most people are more receptive to change when they are brought into the change process early on. They like to be free to determine what change is suitable for them, given their own ways of doing things. They also have to decide whether the proposed change is sufficiently valuable to them to warrant the effort required to make it. They want to satisfy themselves that they can accomplish the change with reasonable or moderate effort and risk. They'll also seek control over how much of the change they'll accept. Ideas or techniques that are off the shelf are the same as clothes off the rack. They usually need alterations and adjustments.

• Most people regard themselves as experts on themselves. No one, they believe, can possibly know their perceptions, feelings, and thoughts as well as they do. Their expertise, therefore, determines how receptive they are to any change that is proposed by someone else.

• Every time you suggest improvements, you have to monitor the change activity. Winding your people up and letting them go isn't effective managing. You may have to follow up your persuasive efforts with frequent reminders that the change will be beneficial. And while a salesperson is trying to change and improve, you need to give feedback. Whatever he or she is doing poorly or not well enough or mistakenly has to be corrected. You are the one to provide that corrective help. If you let a salesperson flounder because you get distracted elsewhere, nothing good will happen. The salesperson will gradually sink back into his or her old ways of selling.

• Don't forget to reinforce new behavior that is successful. Don't assume, as too many managers do, that your salespeople know how much you appreciate what they have done to improve themselves. Rewards don't have to be elaborate. Praise will do just fine. And once in a while, after salespeople have demonstrated that they continue to practice the behaviors, give them some compliments that tell them how gratified you are that they have stuck with it.

• Rationalizing is a very human behavior. Most people like to blame external factors, other people, adverse conditions, and so forth for their failure in an endeavor. Treat the rationalization as you would any prospect's objection: sidestep and keep selling the benefits.

A final word: Just as confused prospects don't buy, confused salespeople won't follow your counsel. Be clear about what you want. Monitor a salesperson's change efforts to make sure he or she works in the right direction. And be clear about rewarding what you wanted when you do in fact get it.

2

Persuading Salespeople to Buy the Change

Selling is persuading. Selling is influencing. Selling is leading. As a field manager and probably former salesperson, you have an advantage over many of your management colleagues: You know how to sell. Most of them who work on the inside don't. And what you know so well is that whenever you want to talk someone into something, you must sell.

The most effective selling is transactional. It's often a negotiating process. As a salesperson, you bring to the transaction an expertise in your product, program, or service. You know its features and, more important, its benefits in a wide range of applications. As a skilled salesperson you also bring a sensitivity to the other person's wants, needs, and agenda. You are articulate; you can clearly express how what you have to offer can benefit the prospect. You also respect what the prospect brings to the transaction. The prospect is somewhat of an expert on his or her needs, knows the business or the practice, and undoubtedly has experience in the kinds of applications you have come to talk about. In short, each of you brings to the transaction certain resources in knowledge, experience, competence, and judgment. When there is a mutual respect for these resources, there is often business done.

There is a parallel in training. Consider your salesperson as your prospect. Generally your salesperson also has resources in experience, skills, and knowledge. If you look at what happens between the two of you as a transaction when you want him or her to improve effectiveness, you'll generally get better results than if you tell rather than sell.

A number of years ago, people talked about transactional analysis (TA), an interest that was fueled by a best-selling book, *Games People Play,* written by psychiatrist Eric Berne. One of the gems of TA that has survived is "I'm OK—you're OK." It's a fundamental approach to interactions between people. You've used it in selling, perhaps without linking it to psychology or a philosophy: When you treat a prospect with respect, you often enjoy reciprocity. Your attitude toward the prospect is this: "There's nothing wrong with you as a person; you just don't know everything there is to know about what we're discussing. I'm here to help close a gap in your knowledge." You adopt the same attitude toward your salesperson: "I know you're not as effective in every situation as you would like to be. Since that's true of all of us, that fact doesn't mean that you are deficient as a person."

When you propose improvement through any form of training, formal or informal, remember that you are working on the salesperson's *wizardry,* not the person. I borrow the term from *The Wizard of Oz,* the book and movie that all of us grew up with. You'll recall that Dorothy, her friends, and her dog, Toto, come face to face with a giant screen and a fearsome face—the wizard's—and a booming, intimidating voice. They shake in terror until Toto runs over to a curtained booth and pulls the curtain back with his teeth to reveal a man working levers and speaking into a microphone. Dorothy, incensed at what she considers to be a fraud, says to the man, "You're a very bad man." To which he responds, "No, I'm a very good man. I'm just a bad wizard." That's what I mean when I say that you are helping your salespeople to perfect their wizardry. You can't afford to blur the distinction between the person and the wizard.

Many managers, unfortunately, don't make the distinction. My favorite story on this subject has to do with a seminar I attended on assertiveness training. There were about forty people in the room. Each of us was asked to stand, give our names, and tell why we were there. Roughly half the participants admitted that they had been sent by their bosses because they were nonassertive, and the rest said they had been enrolled because their bosses felt they were too aggressive. The message they had all received was, "You're not OK. Go get yourself fixed." As a result, probably very little learning and changing occurred at that three-day seminar because people felt resentful and put down.

Training should be presented as a means to become even more effective: Here's how you can become a better wizard.

Recognizing Problems' Degrees of Seriousness

I'm not glossing over the seriousness of the problems salespeople face, but there are degrees of seriousness. At the top of the chart, you may be helping your stars to perfect their wizardry, and what a pleasure that can be. At the bottom, your aim may well be to help ineffective salespeople improve their productivity to a point that is acceptable to you—survival, in other words. And in the middle, the problems can range from very serious to minor.

In determining the seriousness of the problem, you have to start someplace: Something is not as right as it should be and could be, something could be much righter, or something is not right at all. How you convey this message varies: "This is something you absolutely must do," "This is something you are well-advised to do," or "This is something you can do easily and willingly because it will make you a better professional."

The chief considerations in setting goals to overcome problems or deficiencies, major or minor, are that the salespeople be involved in establishing these goals and the means to achieve them and that all discussions about problems and goals be strictly in terms of behavior—never attitudes, motives, or personality characteristics.

Familiar Areas for Change and Improvement

In the preceding section, I use the word *problem* indiscriminately. In some cases you will need to solve performance problems, but for most of your people most of the time, you're not so much dealing in problems as in opportunities. When you see that a salesperson's performance could be improved to become more effective, you're really facing an opportunity to help push that person up a notch or two in competence and skill. In this case, you might not even want to suggest that there is a problem per se.

I once worked with a fine psychologist who trained managers in solving problems. He said that using the *P* word sometimes gets in the way of a solution. People get defensive about who caused the problem, who is to blame. Instead, he would rephrase the question: "We don't like what's happening now. So what would we like in its stead?" Or, "What exists now is not working. What would work?"

Following are a number of selling activity areas in which people can usually achieve some improvement, large or small. You'll recognize most or all of them as familiar, garden variety activities or deficiencies.

Prospecting

- Keeping sloppy or incomplete prospect records
- Failing to update prospect files
- Not regularly adding a minimum of new business prospects
- Using insufficient sources of prospects: directories, newspapers, trade publications, smokestacking, associations, chambers of commerce, etc.
- Having an inadequate mix of prospects—industry, size, location, etc.
- Using direct mail to elicit prospect responses
- Regularly using the telephone to uncover prospects

Time Management and Organization

- Starting earlier, finishing later
- Making lunchtime appointments
- Covering territory erratically or inefficiently
- Scheduling appointments unrealistically, e.g., too many in too short a time, too spaced out
- Not planning alternative drop-in calls between appointments in case of cancellations
- Making better use of the telephone for making appointments in downtime (between appointments or in case of delays or cancellations)

- Doing records work during prime selling time
- Planning travel time to forestall lateness and unnecessary waiting
- Failing to push for appointments at odd times

Telephoning

- Not setting regular times for telephoning for appointments and service
- Using appropriate telephone manner and technique
- Sticking to primary purpose of telephoning—not getting trapped
- Having incomplete records of direct-dial numbers of prospects
- Having a low ratio of successful calls
- Making disorganized telephone presentations
- Permitting diversions from primary purpose and engaging in wasteful small talk
- Controlling tone and pitch of voice
- Talking too fast or too slow
- Not persisting in trying for firm appointments
- Not qualifying the person called as a real prospect
- Failing to control the call
- Handling stalls and objections to an appointment

Interviews

- Pushing for the right place to give a presentation (e.g., not in the lobby)
- Asking questions that elicit useful information
- Failing to qualify the person seen as a buyer, decision maker
- Having difficulty achieving rapport before starting the presentation
- Putting prospects at ease
- Beginning the presentation without a clear sense of the prospect's needs
- Being too willing to present under adverse circumstances
- Relying excessively on technical or product knowledge
- Making presentations that are disorganized or too long

- Insufficient checking for prospect's involvement during the presentation
- Trying to anticipate too many objections in the body of the presentation
- Not pacing the presentation—going too slow or too fast
- Talking to visual material
- Making poor eye contact
- Failing to respond to buying signals
- Presenting disorganized visual material
- Giving rambling or nonresponsive answers to prospect's questions
- Interrupting prospect's questions

Closing

- Having inadequate command of different closing techniques
- Having trouble maintaining silence after a close
- Not making a smooth lead into the close from the presentation
- Failing to ask for commitment
- Making weak or nonclosing statements
- Closing on features rather than benefits
- Giving a sequence of closes

Objections and Stalls

- Being defensive
- Being argumentative
- Listening and relaxing
- Talking excessively in answer to objections
- Failing to close after responding to an objection
- Being too persistent in making callbacks
- Answering an objection before qualifying it
- Being condescending when talking to a prospect
- Not persisting in trying to get a commitment
- Laying insufficient groundwork for callbacks
- Responding in kind to a prospect's rudeness or annoyance
- Answering objections too quickly

Service

- Planning better for service calls
- Doing "missionary" work with users and influentials
- Justifying service calls
- Delaying response to service problems
- Neglecting service follow-up on certain accounts
- Blaming customers for service problems
- Having tact in dealing with problems
- Failing to sell on service calls
- Making service calls during prime selling time

Miscellaneous

- Having poor grooming
- Having poor relationships with home office backup and service people
- Having poor relationships with management
- Failing to maintain accurate and timely reporting
- Not maintaining complete and attractive visual material

Identifying Areas for Improvement

You'll find salespeople doing some of the things on this list when they shouldn't, and not doing others when they should. There are, in general, three ways you can help a salesperson identify areas in which he or she can make improvements. The first, and perhaps the easiest, is to observe the salesperson on a call. Afterward, you offer a bit of curbstone coaching (feedback). (You might want to take a few minutes right now to read the section in Chapter 4 on curbstone coaching.) A second method of discovering barriers to greater effectiveness is to review the salesperson's records. Certain patterns will often display themselves. Finally, you may want to interview the salesperson, to see what he or she regards as a potential area for improvement. Closely related to interviewing is coaching, in which you encourage the salesperson to define a problem and then help the person work toward a solution.

Observing a Salesperson

When you observe a salesperson making sales calls, you have the opportunity to see him or her in action. You notice things the salesperson is or isn't doing. Some of these things are minor and can easily be dealt with in a short curbstone conference. As an example, a salesperson may have difficulty pinning down appointments with some prospects. "He says this is a rush season. Try him after Easter," she complains to you. Neither of you knows whether the stall is well-founded, but you suggest that she experiment with a different approach. For example:

> Some of my busy customers, like you, prefer to see me outside of usual work hours. They feel they have more time to hear what I can offer them without the distractions of the phones and such. Some like to schedule time with me in the early morning before the office opens, or just before they leave in the evening, around six or so. I have one customer who's in his office on Saturday morning and likes to talk then. Perhaps you and I could sit down for a short time around seven thirty in the morning or after six in the evening. Which makes more sense to you?

That doesn't take much rehearsal. It may not always work, but the salesperson has nothing to lose by appending it to her usual requests for appointments, which don't seem to work anyway.

Another illustration of a problem requiring only a minor adjustment is that of jumping on a prospect's questions. Not only does it belittle the value of the questions, but it allows a possibility of mistake: The salesperson may anticipate a meaning that isn't there. The remedy is mechanical: The manager says, "I want you to keep your mouth closed until the prospect is finished, and then I want you to count to three before you say a word." There's very little complication in making sure that the salesperson follows your counsel on the next calls.

Probing a Salesperson's History

Sometimes there are opportunities in a salesperson's productivity reports just awaiting your attention. For example, Jim has failed to cultivate large accounts. His explanation is he feels they take too much time. Instead he goes after small to medium-size companies. In reality, he may lack confidence. His manager can't know that definitely, but he can make sure that he works with Jim on such accounts not only to guide Jim toward good prospecting methods for giant companies but to help him build confidence as he makes inroads.

For a long time Erica has had problems making cold calls. Her manager points out that she needs to supplement the day's appointments with drop-ins to take up slack time. The manager works with Erica to develop some scenarios to anticipate prospects' various reactions to her impromptu calls.

Phil's presentations ramble, and they often consume more time than the prospect has allotted (resulting in overall low activity). Phil often has inadequate time to close. In addition, the presentations are sometimes hard to follow and confuse the prospect. Phil's manager resorts to having Phil write an outline of his principal points, then filling in the rest under the headings. Gradually, through editing, reading the presentation, and role-playing, Phil begins to achieve better organized and shorter interviews.

In each of the above cases, the manager has seen a symptom of a problem in the salesperson's activity reports and has supplemented that observation with knowledge gained through making calls with or querying the salesperson.

Interviewing a Salesperson

The third approach to a self-improvement plan is through interviewing the salesperson. To illustrate, we'll assume that your salesperson, Fred, is very productive and reasonably successful and ambitious. The setting for such an interview should be relaxed, perhaps in the afternoon or evening following the day's work.

You: Well, Fred, today we saw good and very good. But since you're not the kind of person who coasts, let's talk about better, and how I can help you.

Fred: If you mean how to get more business, fine.

You: More business, sure. But also how to make the job easier, maybe even more fun. OK, think about these questions: What are you doing now that you believe you can do better, that you want to do better? Or, what are you doing now that you think gets in the way of doing a better job and that you'd like to get rid of?

Fred [*after thinking a minute*]: I think I can answer both questions. Right now, I'm doing an all right job with my telephoning, but to tell you the truth, I don't like using the phone. I know I have to, but sometimes I just hate to pick up the receiver.

You: I don't think your feeling about the phone is unusual. Tell you what. Tomorrow let's get some phoning in. Let me overhear you, and then maybe I can offer some ideas.

The following morning, Fred comes to your hotel room and sits down to make calls for appointments. You watch and listen. After a time, he turns and asks, "Any comments?" You see a number of ways he can improve his effectiveness. After asking him whether what you've observed is typical, and being told it is, you make some suggestions:

You: I think you need to create some momentum for yourself. Between calls you shuffle your prospect cards as if you're trying to determine which one you should call next. You never really get up to stride. Here's a technique you might want to experiment with: Put your cards into batches of ten or fifteen. Presort. Once you start phoning, you go right through them. It gets to be kind of automatic, and you don't take time to think about how uncomfortable you are. When you've finished a batch, take a short break, then start on the second batch. One thing I like to do that you might like to try. I always like feedback, so I keep a sheet of paper beside the phone. One column is for the calls I make, the second is for calls completed—talking with the right person— and the third is for calls that produce appointments. It's a game I play with myself. Gradually, you'll find that you want to make more calls, and when you see your ratios climbing, you'll feel good about phoning.

When you get back to your office, you write Fred a letter repeating the steps you've described to him. You ask him to let you know each week how he is doing, and suggest that the two of you continue working on his telephone techniques on your next visit.

Coaching and Feedback

When you come out of a sales interview with a salesperson, chances are you both feel the need to talk about what happened, especially if things didn't go well. There are basically two ways to conduct an analysis: through what is commonly termed curbstone coaching (see Chapter 4) or through the more elaborate coaching interview. The difference between the two lies in who does the analysis. When time is short and the fault or mistake is relatively minor, you can simply analyze the situation and give straightforward feedback if you believe that a salesperson will have no problem accepting your analysis. (Giving critical feedback is covered at length in Chapter 4.) The other approach is to follow the guidelines of pure coaching, which leads to a salesperson's self-analysis, with your help in defining the deficiency or area of possible improvement and in finding a solution. Through your questions, you gradually nudge the salesperson to talk about both the problem and what can be done about it.

It's dangerous to make generalizations, but I suggest that with more experienced salespeople, it is better for you to let them self-analyze the problem. Of course, sometimes the criticism is so minor that it hardly warrants analysis. For example, "It helps if you place the pen close to the contract. You kept it to yourself. Next time, slide it over so that it's easy to pick up." Or, "You didn't take a few seconds to check your briefcase to see that the right catalog was where it should have been. That's why you got so distracted when you looked for it during the presentation." Or, "It seemed to me that you jumped too fast to answer her questions. In fact, once you didn't even let her finish. What I recommend is that you take care to let the prospect finish what she wants to say, take a moment to think about it—that's very complimentary—and then answer. Here's the formula: wait, listen, think, answer."

In short, if a salesperson is quite experienced and competent, if the problem is minor or requires an immediate solution, and if time is of the essence, you can probably accomplish your goal by straightforward feedback. But if the deficiency is more complicated and will involve some learning or relearning, and if there is time to do an analysis, then try coaching. Insist that the salesperson identify the problem and perhaps even suggest the solution, or the beginning of one.

Coaching often compliments a salesperson and enhances his or her sense of professionalism. The salesperson feels like more of a partner in the improvement process. In addition, he or she will be less resistant to your counsel after having had a role in problem identification. A note of caution, however. New salespeople may not have the self-confidence or be comfortable enough with you to participate in the coaching process. When you sense that possibility, be straightforward, give feedback, and be as matter-of-fact about it as you can.

Following are some coaching scenarios that illustrate the above.

Coaching Scenario One

Over lunch, George says to his manager, Mel: "I'm getting a lot of price objections lately."

Mel: What's a lot?

George: Maybe three, four a week. I never used to have that many.

Mel: Well, what do you think may account for the sudden increase?

George: A couple of reasons. People are trimming costs. They want to squeeze everything out of the dollar they can. And I guess they don't think we're competitive.

Mel: Do you think that?

George: I've had no hard evidence. Do you find that around the region?

Mel: No. Are you doing something that triggers the price objection?

George: I don't know. You heard me this morning. What do you think?

Mel: That first presentation. Remember when Hancock mentioned how the costs of raw materials kept going up, early in the presentation? What did you do?

George: I showed him the graph, that rises haven't been in excess of the consumer price index.

Mel: That was your graph, wasn't it? Do you use it often?

George: Well, yeah, I made it because I was beginning to hear about how our prices are out of line.

Mel: So, if someone brings up price during the presentation, that's how you deal with it. You bring out the graph and try to prove otherwise.

George: Right.

Mel: And you didn't used to do that. What'd you do then?

George: It didn't seem to be such a big deal.

Mel: Before you made the graph, you didn't get an unusual number of price objections. Now that you use it, you seem to get many more. What might that tell you?

George: That maybe I'm getting defensive. I'm jumping the gun. It goes back to the Secundum account. I worked my tail off for that business, and they told me I lost it because my prices were higher. That's when I began to use my graph. I thought I could head off the problem.

Mel: And what's happened?

George: I may be creating it. That's a laugh.

Mel: So what's the solution?

George: You know, I've suckered myself. I used to have a rule that nobody could get me to talk about price until I was ready. I'd just step right around it if it came up during the presentation. But now I'm gun-shy. I'm trying to head it off, and instead I'm planting it in the prospect's mind.

Mel: Could be. I've never really thought the price objection was about price. It's about value. The prospect is flashing you a signal: "I'm not sold." So when you sidetrack yourself to talk about the price, you're not hitting the prospect's target. Tell you what, George. This afternoon, try to keep the price out of the discussion on the rest of the calls. At the end of the day, I want you to give me a presentation, and I'll bring up price. Let's see how you used to handle it. We'll role-play it. And then join me for breakfast in the morning, and we'll try it again. That ought to get you back into your old practice.

Coaching Scenario Two

Sitting in the car following a call, Jennie exclaims to her boss, Robin, "Damn, I really thought I had him. He was with me all during the presentation, and then he pulled back when I asked him to buy."

Robin: When do you think it went wrong?

Jennie: When I closed, I was sure he would pick up the pen and sign. But he didn't, which flabbergasted me, because he'd been giving me buying signals all the way through. Didn't he?

Robin: I thought so.

Jennie: So, tell me. You were listening and watching. What happened?

Robin: Let's compare notes. Up to the time you asked him to buy, we both thought he would go along. When did you first have a doubt?

Jennie: When he didn't make a move. He was hesitating.

Robin: What did you do then?

Jennie: I reminded him of the thirty-day trial that protected him. Cancel within thirty days, return everything, no questions asked, no obligation.

Robin: Then what happened?

Jennie: He said he couldn't make the decision until after the first of the month. He'd have to check his budget and talk with his partner. So, I call him back next month. But I think I lost him.

Robin: I don't know. But you didn't get him today, and we both thought you would. How come the thirty-day guarantee didn't work, do you suppose?

Jennie: I don't know.

Robin: OK, I'm going to push this. Why don't you have a clue?

Jennie: I'm not following you. How could I know?

Robin: But you must have assumed that he had forgotten about the trial period, because that's what you threw at him.

Jennie: I didn't know. At that point I was looking for anything to push him over the edge. You're not saying anything. I guess you don't agree.

Robin: Well, it didn't work, did it? What does that tell you?

Jennie: It tells me that I should have kept my mouth shut. I talked when I should have listened.

Robin: It's true that you can't risk very much when you stay silent. You asked for the order. The ball was in his court. He knew he had to do something. And what did you do?

Jennie: I took him off the hook. I broke the silence. If I hadn't, he probably would have told me why he wasn't buying. That's one of the first things I learned as a saleswoman.

Coaching Scenario Three

Trevor is relaxing at the end of a long day of working with Eve, whose productivity has been acceptable but not terribly impressive. Trevor suspects that she is having problems getting firm appointments. "What would you say, Eve, is your greatest concern at the moment, the thing that is preventing you from getting the results you want?"

Eve: That's easy. The telephone. I'm not comfortable with it.

Trevor: Let's talk about it. What kinds of problems do you have with it?

Eve: What don't I have? It scares me to death. I have to push myself to pick up the receiver. And I'm sure that my discomfort really comes through.

Trevor: Do you think that if you were better at using the telephone you would pick up more appointments?

Eve: I know I would.

Trevor: OK, let's run through your usual experience on the telephone. When do you make most of your calls? How many do you make at a time? What causes you the most discomfort?

Eve: Well, I think the biggest problem is getting started, getting over the threshold. Then I have a lot of anxiety trying to get through to the person I want to talk with. And I stumble. The words sometimes just don't come out right.

Trevor: What kind of success do you have now? How many appointments do you get out of how many calls?

Eve: Oh, maybe one appointment for every twelve or fifteen calls.

Trevor: That's not a disaster. But it would help you if you could get that ratio down to one appointment for every, say, eight calls. Practice on me. Call me as if I were a cold prospect. How would you conduct the call?

*　　*　　*

Trevor: Let me give you some feedback. You went through three calls with me, and all three were somehow different. Yet the objective was the same for all three: to get an appointment. What's your comment on that?

Eve: Well, I suppose maybe I'm reinventing the wheel each time.

Trevor: That's a pretty good analysis. It takes a lot of energy to find new things to say to different prospects. Don't you think you might save some of that energy if you knew in advance what you were going to say to each one? No surprises. No innovating. No searching.

Eve: What would that be?

Trevor: How about a brief script? Something you could follow, not slavishly, but something that would always tell you where you could go.

Eve: Would you help me?

Trevor: Of course. After we do that, and after you've become comfortable with it, we'll go to step two: helping you make more calls than you do now. In other words, we start with quality, then work on quantity. Make sense?

Coaching Scenario Four

For a minute or two in the car after the interview, Rich is silent. Then he turns to his boss, Gerry, and says wryly, "Well, you certainly have to say I'm persistent. I closed that guy time after time. I didn't get the order, but I sure hung in there."

Gerry: Yep, that you did.

Rich: OK, now tell me, what did I do wrong?

Gerry: No, first you tell me what you think you might have done wrong.

Rich: Aha, caught you. You really do believe I screwed it up.

Gerry: I'm not going to play this little game. Do you think you screwed it up? If you do, then tell me how.

Rich: All right. I thought my first close was very strong. After that, I sensed I got weaker and weaker.

Gerry: I agree. Now, do you have any thoughts about why you seemed to lose ground?

Rich: I'm not sure. I guess I wasn't very imaginative.

Gerry: Meaning?

Rich: Well, as I look back on it, I think I kept saying pretty much the same thing over and over again. I wasn't giving him fresh reasons to buy.

Gerry: Rich, I think that's right on. I felt that way too. What was your closing technique? How would you describe it?

Rich: Well, I summed up some of the benefits that I thought he would get, and asked for the order.

Gerry: True. You went through the summary close immediately following your presentation. I thought that was good. But the second time, and the third, and the fourth, you gave him essentially a summary. If he didn't buy into it the first time, what made you believe he was going to go for it the second, and so on?

Rich: As I said, not much imagination. I was desperate.

Gerry: Why? What about the other closes you've been trained in? I sat there wondering why you didn't give him a minor point choice, like saying: "Do you want to get this started on the first of the month or, listen, I could really try to get it going on the twentieth, if you want." Or you could have tried penalty and reassurance: Look what's going to happen if you don't start this. Or capitalizing on the objection. You handled the objections fine. You finally found out why he didn't want to buy, but you didn't qualify it. You didn't meet it head on. Remember how you do it: If we take care of this problem, are you ready to go? Instead, you kept presenting your summary.

Rich: I'm getting rusty.

Gerry: You're not using your resources. Look, tonight I want you to get out the sales manual and review various ways to close. Then I want you to write down how you might have used each one on this prospect. Bring it along with you tomorrow, and we'll talk about it.

Persuading a Resistant Person to Change

If a salesperson is performing reasonably well, you might get a bit of resistance to your ongoing efforts to improve his or her effectiveness. It does little good to use your "I'm the boss" tone when a salesperson is generally performing up to your standards. However, suppose what you observe in the person's production are some major stumbling blocks, such as mediocre competence on the telephone in getting confirmed appointments, or a presentation that has too much of a winging-it quality, or a tendency not to qualify callbacks sufficiently, or a hit-or-miss record in handling objections.

Here's the case of a manager who has on previous visits to Angela's territory suggested that her head-on approach to responding to a prospect's objections may be depriving her of some business. But Angela, who sees herself as a reasonably competent closer, always nodded and said nothing to those suggestions. Her manager, Bob, assumed that she was giving him the response he wanted and that she'd do things her way after he left, which she did. On a return visit, Bob sits through a call in which Angela unsuccessfully presses for an order. In the few minutes before the next call, Bob attempts a bit of curbstone coaching and selling:

Bob: How do you feel about the call, Angela?

Angela: I thought I had him. I know I gave a damn fine presentation, and he was really with it all the way.

Bob: I agree with you. It was a very good story. Why do you think he didn't buy?

Angela: Beats me. He seemed worried about the extra price, but I think I demolished his worries about that. Boy, was I surprised when he told me to call him next month, that he wanted to think about it.

Bob: I can imagine how frustrated you are. It looked as if it were going so well.

Angela: Oh, and how.

Bob is being very responsive to Angela, getting her assessment of what went on and empathizing with her feelings of disappointment and frustration. He waits for her to speak.

Angela: What really gets me are the times, like just now, when I feel I'm cooking, and then I walk out wondering why I didn't get the order. It seemed so close. If I know I blew it, it hurts, but not as bad as when I can't figure out why it didn't go right.

Bob: How often have you had that kind of experience lately?

Angela: Oh, not often.

Bob: Just give me an idea. I know it doesn't happen often. You're a very fine salesperson. But say over the last month, how many times have you walked away like today wondering why it slipped away from you?

Angela: Maybe three, four times.

Bob: You're right, that's not often. Still, I know you well enough. You don't like to lose any. If I didn't know you so well, I'd think that you were pressing so hard because you were thinking this is the order that puts food on the table. And without it . . .

Angela [*laughs*]: I don't give up easily.

Bob: I know. Maybe I can help. You know, I sit there watching. Now and then something flashes through my head, an idea that might reduce that three or four.

Angela: All right.

Bob: Listen, I'm not handing down the truth from on high. Nothing like that. But since you hate to lose, more than anybody I know, maybe you'd be interested in experimenting a bit.

Angela: Go on.

Bob is following good selling practices. He's probing to confirm his assumption that Angela's pride in herself will open the door to his "product." Now he qualifies:

Bob: I think I may have some suspicion about what happened. After all, you were in the middle of the whole thing. You were pretty busy. Here's my question to you: Where do you think it might have started to slip away from you?

Angela: Well, when he brought up that thing about paying us more than his present supplier for the same thing. Only I showed him that it wasn't the same thing, that our controls are more adaptable, and that they last longer than the industry average. That we were actually going to cost him less over the long haul.

Bob: And then what did he say?

Angela: He brought up the thing about wanting to think it over and would I call him next month. A stall.

Bob: And you kept on selling. You had the facts and figures. It was a good job.

Angela: It couldn't have been. I didn't get a yes.

Bob: How sure are you that price was the real objection?

Angela: I asked him, and he confirmed it.

Bob: But you answered his price objection. Still no sale. And you're frustrated.

Angela: What do you think I should have done?

Bob: Let's talk in terms of what you could have done, I don't know about should have. You closed hard. It was good. Then he objected to the cost. You came back fast. You were firm. You were confident. You were on top of it. But he didn't go with you. Let's assume that price wasn't the real objection. What do you think it might have been?

Angela: I don't know. I was so sure he was leveling with me.

Bob: One thing you could have done was take a little longer to find out whether price was the real thing. There wasn't a rush in there.

Angela: I know, you like to sidestep. But I've been awfully good at smelling out the real thing and getting rid of it.

Bob: True, except for today, and three or four other times. All I'm suggesting is that we experiment a bit and see whether we cut down on the times you walk out wondering what the devil happened. Are you game? What do you have to lose?

With utmost sensitivity, Bob has sold his product to Angela. He wants her to use a technique for handling objections that involves her accepting the initial objection without agreeing with it, and then going on to sell more benefits, to close again. If she closes, say, three times, and the objection remains the same, she can then respond to it directly.

The Five Steps in Selling

There are five steps in a sales transaction, and Bob in the above example used them all. Here they are:

1. Know your product.
2. Know your prospect.
3. Involve your prospect.
4. Ask for action.
5. Be prepared to handle opposition.

Bob knew from the outset that he had a product to sell: a different method for handling objections. But he couldn't simply spring it on Angela, because he suspected that she would resist it as she had in the past. So he probed to uncover her needs and wants. Angela is a very proud professional. She sets high standards for herself. She doesn't like to lose, especially when she doesn't understand precisely why she lost. Once he had confirmed her strong need, Bob moved on to step 3. He involved her by asking her to relive what happened and by suggesting that, since her way hadn't worked, there might have been an option. As he anticipated, she threw up an objection: She found his sidestepping techniques to be a lot of trouble. He gently reminded her that her usual way hadn't worked. Then he asked for action: Try my suggestion. It might work. What do you have to lose? Here's my product, and here's how you can use it.

Taking Things One at a Time

There may be times, as you make calls with salespeople, that you see many areas in which they could improve. So-called laundry lists are not workable. Dragging out six or seven things to do may overwhelm them. Concentrate on one thing at a time, unless the behaviors are slight and easily changed.

I still recall a nightmarish situation during a sales call that I made in California with a salesman. The program he was describing to the prospect consisted of reports and newsletters. Instead of merchandising the concept behind and the purpose of each report, he reduced the presentation to selling pieces of paper. He just kept pushing the paper across the desk at the prospect as he described the features: "Your people will get this every other week. And this comes out every quarter." It was a lackluster presentation. But what really horrified me was that he was trying to head off what had apparently been a frequent objection: "I don't have time to read all this." So as he shoveled each piece of paper across the desk, he would add, "You can see, this is not too much to read." After a while my horror subsided and I began to entertain myself by counting the number of times he made that statement. I also thought that if the prospect hadn't worried about reading time before, he surely would now. Then a terrible thought crossed my mind: The salesman was going to ask me if I had any suggestions for improvement, and I flirted briefly with the thought of telling him to find another line of work. Finally I decided to tell him about the reading admonition.

He did indeed ask me for my thoughts, and I replied, after taking a minute to impress him how seriously I took his question, "Are you aware of how many times you assured the prospect that he wouldn't find this too much to read?" He looked startled and shook his head no. "I counted twelve, and then I stopped counting." That mistake was easily remedied, but there were too many other problems.

Pick one area that you believe is relatively easy to remedy, succeed with that, and then go on to another. If you are unfortunate enough to have a salesperson such as the one above, who seems hopelessly in over his head, more drastic solutions are in order.

Being Sensitive

In enlisting your salesperson in a change effort, you need to be accepting. The person has a difficulty, has created a barrier, or seems unaware of what he or she is not doing. If you want to create a partnership to make a change, it's not a good idea to express amazement or bafflement over the salesperson's performance. "What were you trying to do when you did that?" Or, "How'd you ever get the idea that that's the way to handle that objection?" Or, "Gee, I can't believe you let that one pass you by." Expressing such incredulity or sarcasm is a fast way to turn someone off. They're hardly going to be eager to listen to your advice.

Another problem that managers create for themselves is that of projecting. "I can do that," they say or think, "therefore she can." Maybe. Maybe not. But when a salesperson asks for your help, the last thing he or she wants to hear is, "Oh, that's easy." Or, "What's difficult about that?" Such remarks belittle.

Handling an Overambitious Salesperson

Some managers are reluctant to ask subordinates to help set their own achievement goals because, they argue, subordinates tend to set goals too low. Actually, in many cases, the opposite is true. When a salesperson is turned on to the opportunity to increase productivity through an improvement action plan, he or she may set the goals unusually high. For example, you're looking for a modest increase in sales calls, say from an average of fifteen a week to eighteen. You may be startled to hear your salesperson say, "Let's make it twenty. I know I can do that." Maybe. And you might be tempted to let him have a shot at it. Can it hurt? Yes, it can. Better to shoot for seventeen or eighteen and make that than to strive for twenty and consistently fall short. Goals that are not seen as attainable demotivate. After a while of being short, the salesperson will probably give up. Thus, it's better to make the change incremental. If he achieves the eighteen in a month or so and is encouraged, you can edge the goal a little higher. That's what they do for jumpers on the track. You keep raising the pole a bit at a time.

Using Learning Contracts

The change you want may be small, it may be easy to accomplish, and it may be achieved in a short time. Still, treat it seriously. Make it a contract between you and the salesperson. When you treat it with respect, the salesperson is likely to do so as well. Follow these four steps to set up a learning contract:

1. Set a goal. For example, to increase the average number of calls, or get a higher ratio of commitments on the telephone, or give a more concise presentation.
2. Define your role as coach, observer, mentor, trainer, and above all, as partner in the process.
3. Ensure that the new knowledge or skill is applied under real-life conditions. You have to assume responsibility for seeing that this is done. It's part of your contract.
4. When the skill has been successfully applied and the goal has been achieved, make sure you fulfill the contract: Reinforce the new competence.

Learning contracts can be very informal, although nothing says that you can't tie them down in a letter or a memo. But whether formal or informal, they must be respected and, as far as possible, completed. Otherwise, such contracts lose their power to influence and to bind.

Training in Meetings

Using a meeting to help in the ongoing upgrading of your salespeople has its pluses and minuses. Let's look at the positives first:

+ *Cross-fertilization.* Some of the best exchanges in a meeting are those between peers. When they can role-play, demonstrate, or simply discuss ideas and techniques during a meeting or during social times, they can inspire and educate one another. You may double the benefit for them and for you.

+ *Team building.* A good meeting can increase the sense of membership on a team, which in turn can inspire your salespeople to want to help one another and contribute to the team's success.

+ *Increased learning for you.* There may be some feedback about the company, or the home office staff, or policies and procedures that an individual might not give to you, out of the fear that it's not important enough or inappropriate. But in a group, where there is support, the knowledge that others feel the same way encourages openness. Of course, you may not like what you hear, but you probably need to know it.

+ *Efficient transfer of information.* If you have ten salespeople in one place, you can cover a lot of information a lot faster than saying the same thing ten times over. And theoretically, everyone gets the same information, although not everyone hears it the same.

+ *A break from routine.* Selling involves pressure and stress. A pleasant two or three days, preferably in a congenial locale, can revivify.

Now let's consider the negative side of training meetings:

− *Less individual attention.* The meeting may be an efficient but not necessarily an effective exchange. People have varying needs and concerns, and a meeting easily takes on the character of one size fits all. You have to take pains to make sure that everyone does indeed hear and understand what you want them to.

— *Fast follow-up.* If there is to be learning, you'll have to make sure there is application and feedback on the job. Drilling, role-playing, and demonstrating during the session are fine, but what happens back in the territory is what counts. The pressure will be on you to move around the territories fast to make sure that the content of the meeting doesn't fade away.

— *Monopoly by your stars.* Your stars are probably quite good at competing with other companies, and that means they can compete with you. Big talkers and forceful personalities can easily take over meetings. Now and then you'll have a high producer who loves to try to shoot down conventional wisdom, including your advice to the sales force. Of course, you can try to muzzle him or her before the session, but that is somewhat censorial and conspiratorial. It may backfire. You also don't want to embarrass anyone in public.

— *Reinforcement of inferior status.* This is a subtle consideration, but if you have a salesperson who is borderline or below in performance, having to mix with obviously successful people may tend to reinforce his or her worries that success is elusive. The salesperson may go home quite dispirited. On the other hand, if he or she is a performance problem and decides to bow out voluntarily, that could save a lot of trouble for you.

— *Out of the field and away from the family.* If you schedule the meeting during the week, you create pressure on your salespeople by taking them away from their selling. If you hold it over a weekend, you cut into their personal and family time, which may annoy some of them.

What's a Good Meeting?

A good meeting that people like and learn from is seldom a spontaneous affair. You want your meeting to be efficient and effective: everything done expeditiously with the results you want.

Here are some suggestions for increasing the impact and the value of your meeting:

• *Make it focused.* Some salespeople may like the break or the opportunity to socialize. But most, if they are highly motivated, will expect you to make clear from the outset why they should attend. Some managers are coy, suggesting to their people that all will be revealed in time. For one weekend meeting I was expected to attend, the sales staff was so coy that I never could find out why we were gathered there. I still don't know, but I remember that my mood progressed from puzzlement to annoyance to fury. That was not a cost-effective meeting as far as I was concerned. The more focused you are and the more value you can attach to the meeting up-front, the less likely that you'll run into resistance and resentment.

• *Don't overload.* There's a distinct temptation to say, "We have them for only three days. Let's give them everything we can." But people generally have a limited capacity to process information in a short time. You're much more likely to succeed if you limit the objectives. There's an added factor that impedes the effectiveness of long, concentrated meetings: the concentration span. Most people, it's fair to say, can pay maximum attention to what is said for about sixty to ninety minutes, at most. After that, weariness sets in and they are easily distracted. Keep your sessions short; provide many breaks. You'll accomplish much more than if you plow on for two or three hours at a time.

• *Keep the entire meeting brief.* There's no magic attached to three days, which is an average length. Your salespeople will be a bit antsy about being away from the front, so schedule the meeting for only as long as you need.

• *Provide time to talk about their concerns.* Trainers usually construct a wish list at the outset of a session. It's a good idea for you too. In the first few minutes of the meeting, go around the room and ask the participants what they hope to carry away at the end. Of course, by this time, you should already have made it clear what the objectives and the scope of your planned meeting are. Many of their responses in the round-robin will be related to your objectives, but some will probably bring up other concerns.

You would be well-advised to set some time aside to deal with them. You might say, "We have a couple of hours on Saturday when we're going to address these issues." Or if the concern is primarily that of one person, you can always respond, "Don, why don't you and I sit down over a drink at five and talk about this?"

You don't want to surrender control of the meeting entirely, but at the same time you want to handle people's worries, concerns, and suggestions. If, however, during the round-robin a particular matter that you don't want to deal with in the present forum keeps coming up, make it clear that you won't be addressing it. It is advisable to tell your salespeople when and how you will eventually address the issue, but it's also essential that they rid themselves of any expectation of covering it in the meeting. In short, do not allow expectations to rise that you cannot meet. Otherwise people go away from the meeting annoyed and frustrated. Those feelings can spoil your hopes for a good outcome.

After the Meeting

Good feelings and knowledge born in a meeting can dissipate quickly. You'll probably want to visit each salesperson after the meeting or delegate that task to someone else: a home office person, other experienced salesperson, or your assistant. But meantime you can keep the spirit going with letters and phone calls to those who attended the training meeting.

KEY TO CHAPTER 3

A partnership connotes a joint effort toward mutually accepted goals. As manager, you want your salespeople to commit themselves to a continuing program of increased effectiveness. And you believe that your salespeople are equally interested in sharpening their skills, building their competence, and growing professionally to achieve ever better results for themselves, for you, and for the company.

But a partnership implies trust and mutual respect. It isn't simply declared; it grows. It is nourished by the environment in which it takes root. Although you are the boss and your salespeople are subordinates who report to you, you can form partnerships with them as long as they believe you are interested in their well-being as well as in your own. They need to know that you are invested in their success as much as in your own. You convey these important messages through the way you relate to your salespeople, through the atmosphere that you create in the region, division, or district, through the opportunities you provide them in achieving their goals and enjoying their rewards for achievement.

Following is a self-assessment checklist that reveals how you relate, the atmosphere that you create, and the rewards you point them toward. The assessment defines your managerial style and suggests how strongly you regard your salespeople as partners and assets, to themselves as well as to you. The more strongly your people regard themselves as part of your team, the more completely you will be able to enlist them in the continuing development of team excellence.

Assessing Your Working Style With Salespeople

Which of the following statements characterize how well you work with salespeople, the manner in which you regard them, and the climate you try to create in your district, region, or division?

	Yes	No
1. As far as possible, I prefer to emphasize a more horizontal relationship with the salespeople who work with me—a partnership, a team membership—rather than the traditional vertical relationship of boss and subordinate.	_____	_____

	Yes	No

2. I believe that my salespeople bring to this partnership certain strengths, resources, knowledge, and experience that I must respect and that can be applied to building a more effective sales group. _____ _____

3. In my region there is a fairly wide-open flow of information—up, down, and across. _____ _____

4. The salespeople I work with perceive themselves as members of a unified team. _____ _____

5. I believe that I have an obligation to my salespeople to help them become as effective as possible and to fulfill their potential as sales professionals. _____ _____

6. Although I encourage my salespeople to be competitive and to want to win, I am certain that they are interested in the company's well-being. _____ _____

7. I actively and frequently solicit my salespeople for help in finding solutions to sales problems and in developing techniques that will enable them to sell more effectively. _____ _____

8. Although I encourage a full schedule of sales activity, I firmly believe that salespeople should be evaluated on the basis of the results they achieve from that activity. _____ _____

9. The long-term development of my salespeople is as high a priority as their short-term results. _____ _____

10. The salespeople who work with me generally regard criticism as contributing to their improved effectiveness. _____ _____

11. I seek information from my salespeople on the operation of the company and of our region, since I believe that their perceptions of what we do and how we do it are as important as mine. _____ _____

12. In dealing with salespeople's performance problems, I'm less interested in assigning blame than I am in helping them find alternative behaviors that will benefit us all. _____ _____

	Yes	No
13. I concern myself with morale in my region, but I'm far more concerned with motivation.	_____	_____
14. My salespeople feel free to send critical messages to me and to higher management.	_____	_____
15. I prefer to use persuasive techniques to obtain salespeople's collaboration and commitment.	_____	_____
16. When my salespeople get together with me, the atmosphere is characterized by openness.	_____	_____
17. Generally I believe that my salespeople are eager to achieve greater effectiveness in selling and to grow as professionals and people.	_____	_____
18. It is very important to enlist the participation of salespeople in setting performance goals.	_____	_____
19. My salespeople trust that I will not intentionally do anything that might create a barrier to their achieving the results they seek.	_____	_____
20. The key people in my region know that I value them for the quality of the work they do and that my rewards are based on performance.	_____	_____

Analysis

Just as your salespeople build relationships with their customers, you as manager build relationships with them. These relationships largely determine how they view you—as a boss, a resource, a business or even a personal friend, a guide, and perhaps most of all, a partner. Their perceptions of you and your role affect their willingness to entrust their growth and progress to you, to accept your counsel and suggestions, and to risk having you monitor their activities.

Many of the statements that you reviewed and checked off in the preceding self-assessments are rooted in the research of an outstanding social scientist, the late Rensis Likert, who was director of the Institute for Social Research at the University of Michigan. Through the years,

Likert surveyed managers throughout the United States to discover what kinds of organizational climates and functions lead to greater organizational effectiveness—the ability of its members to work together toward the achievement of the organization's goals. Likert concluded that the most effective companies were those he called System 4: Participative Group. (The other three systems are Exploitative Authoritative, Benevolent Authoritative, and Consultative, all reflecting a strong and fixed vertical relationship of boss and subordinate.) Here is a description of System 4 that appears in an earlier book of mine (*How People Work Best*, Executive Enterprises, 1988):

> Management trusts employees, regards them as working willingly toward the achievement of organizational objectives. People are motivated by rewards. At all levels they are involved in discussing and deciding those issues that are important to them. Communication is quite accurate and goes up, down, and across. Goals are not ordered from on high but are set with the participation of the people who will have to work to achieve them.

Thus, if you are working to build and guide a winning sales team—a supportive motivated group whose members are all moving in the same direction—you can confidently accept Likert's System 4 as a model. Yours is a true partnership with your salespeople. The more effective you can help them to be, the better the team you'll manage. Your relationship, as statement 2 in the preceding checklist implies, is a partnership because you recognize that your salespeople bring to it various resources that strengthen the entire work group. These same resources can be valuable in finding solutions to problems that exist in the company and the region and in developing techniques for selling more profitably.

Statement 8 reflects a managerial value that is surprisingly hard to find in U.S. companies. Without realizing it, many managers have fallen into rewarding inputs and activities rather than outputs and results. In fact, many employee appraisal systems emphasize inputs, such as when they rate employees on taking initiative, working cooperatively, managing resources, and so on. What's most important in these categories is what happens as a result of the various skills being appraised. Ironically, some salespeople also deceive themselves into believing that an active week of making calls and giving presentations is equal to coming up with the orders. If you evaluate your salespeople in terms of the results of their efforts, your judgments are sound and your advice on improving will be much more to the point. And your salespeople will have confidence in your evaluations, because they know that they are based on objective and measurable evidence.

Statement 11 is more vital to success than a lot of managers realize. One key indicator of the health of a company is how closely the perception of the people at the bottom matches that of those at the top in matters of operation, mission, goals, and so forth. People at the top often congratulate themselves on how well the company is thriving, but if the people lower down don't share that enthusiasm, something is very wrong. You can therefore take frequent measurings of the health of your operation by actively seeking the perceptions of your salespeople: "How are we doing, in your estimation?"

Morale, as mentioned in statement 13, is given high priority by many managers. But in fact, we have no reliable evidence that there is a close relationship between morale and motivation. You will see organizations and departments in which people work effectively even when their morale is low. You'll also encounter work groups in which there is much happiness without much productivity. All we really know about happy people is that they are happy. They don't necessarily work better, in the short term anyway, than unhappy people. But if you concentrate on motivation, you are likely to help your folks achieve job satisfaction, which is closely linked to commitment. Good morale often follows.

As you head into the rest of this book, remember two sets of five steps. The first five steps have to do with enhancing the motivation of the people who report to and work with you:

1. Tell your salespeople what you expect them to do (regularly).
2. Make the work valuable to them (by seeing to it that they get out of it what they want).
3. Make the work doable (by training, coaching, guiding, advising).
4. Give critical feedback as they try to do what you expect (and remember that they need that feedback to perform better).
5. Reward them when they have performed as expected if you want them to continue to do well.

The second set of five steps has to do with the persuasive process:

1. Know your product (what you are selling to your salespeople and what's in it for them).

2. Know your prospect (that's your salesperson) and his or her needs and wants.
3. Involve your prospect (show why what you are selling will benefit him or her).
4. Ask for action (get a commitment to the change or the improvement).
5. Be prepared to handle opposition (your salespeople may not always feel that you deserve the order).

If you keep these important and basic realities in mind as you work in partnership with your salespeople, you should have no serious problems in pushing your team to the top.

3

Playing a Partnership Role in Making the Change Successful

You'll recall that value and expectation of success are the two essentials in motivation. What you ask of a salesperson must produce a result (reward) that is of sufficient value to motivate him or her to do it. But the salesperson has to feel reasonably confident that he or she will be successful in achieving the goal.

You can supply both the value and the means for the salesperson to feel confident, because you have internal (from them) and external (from you) rewards to work with. And you can enhance a salesperson's ability to be successful in making the change or improvement. You are mentor, teacher, trainer, coach, adviser, and confidant—an all-around resource to the salesperson. More important is that you encourage the salesperson to see you as a partner in the change effort.

There are certain steps you can take to help a salesperson be more comfortable with attempting to improve his or her competence. First, remember the advice I offered earlier: Keep the change incremental and focused. Generally, people don't improve their effectiveness in selling by taking great leaps or by advancing on a broad front. If the change is somewhat complex and extensive, be sure to set a number of subgoals. "I think you're capable of doubling your activity and your volume, but of course you won't do that all at once. So let's plan it in steps. The first quarter, we'll aim for 15 percent improvement. Once you've accomplished that, perhaps the second quarter we'll go for 20 percent." And so on.

The second recommendation is to make the schedule realistic, and be prepared to lengthen it if the change effort becomes burdensome or iffy. You can hardly expect a salesperson to learn and apply several closing techniques in one day. You might say, "I want you to practice these closers, and I'll schedule time with you in about a month. We'll see how far you've come." When you return, you may find that he or she is not progressing as well as you'd like. So you set another month to practice and learn. In motivation, we often find that people's expectation of being successful in reaching a goal can be reduced by a schedule that the person perceives as too tight. It creates pressure. The person suffers demotivation. So you open up the schedule, relieving the pressure.

The third bit of advice I offer is to make yourself reasonably accessible. Nothing is as discouraging to a salesperson as having a manager rather airily set some goals and then depart, leaving the hapless salesperson to wonder how he or she is to proceed. You might say, "We'll work on this in the calls we make today, and then you can let me know in a week or so how everything is working out. If you want me to come back to work with you for another day, I'll schedule a return visit. In the meantime, if you run into problems that you're not sure how to handle, call me. If I'm on the road, my secretary will find me. I'll call you back." Being available to your salespeople can increase their self-confidence enormously.

Fourth, work with the salesperson to develop sales techniques that go with the grain of his or her personality and selling style. Some salespeople are excellent at building rapport with small talk before and during the presentation. The small talk relaxes the prospects and opens them up to the sales story. Other salespeople are not comfortable making inconsequential conversation. They are more oriented toward getting right into the obvious selling. Such people may benefit from training in asking various kinds of questions instead, since good questions can be very effective in building a relationship between buyer and seller. Some salespeople are superb at thinking "on their feet." They're adaptable and flexible. But others must have almost everything programmed. In this case, you should help them develop well-rehearsed options. Some people seem to be natural charmers who warm up any room they enter. Others find it difficult to be spontaneous and to relate to others quickly. In short, the idea is to encourage the salesperson to join with you in developing ways to change that are natural to him or her. It's usually not a good idea to try to use someone else's mode of operation.

The fifth recommendation is to be prepared to listen patiently. It's comforting and reassuring for your salespeople to know that you will lend a friendly, understanding ear. By listening, you increase the probability that you will learn more about how salespeople perceive their strengths and you will be better able to build on these strengths. Salespeople who encounter problems increasing their effectiveness sometimes need a chance to talk openly and thoroughly to work out a solution. You may sometimes find that the greatest assistance you can render is being prepared to listen.

Finally, help your salespeople learn how to analyze their success with the change efforts. Your analysis based on your observations is useful, since as an outside observer, you'll often see things happening in the sales interview that a salesperson doesn't. But salespeople must develop analytical skills that they can apply all the time. The analyses should cover successes as well as failures. Recall the coaching scenarios in the preceding chapter, and use those techniques to help your salespeople build their analytical skills.

Role-Playing

You can provide a good model for the new desired behavior through role-playing with your salespeople. The best time to hold a role-playing session is just before a salesperson has a chance to practice it on a prospect. Then after the attempted application, you can give feedback and practice it again before the next call. The immediacy ensures that the practice is still fresh in the salesperson's mind when he or she practices it with a customer.

What I'd like you to do, Stan, is to offer an objection after I close you. Then I want you to watch and listen to everything

I do. Then we'll turn it around, and I'll play the customer. You can emulate me.

When Stan throws you an objection, you can go through the usual objection-handling process. You relax physically, sitting back in your chair. You keep your facial expression attentive but free from frowns. You ask a question about the objection, encouraging Stan to elaborate on it. While he talks, you listen carefully. Then you accept: "I can certainly see that that is a consideration with you." Then you move on to sell more benefits, closing again. When you've finished your demonstration, ask Stan to tell you what he saw and heard. What he doesn't remember or didn't notice, you fill in. Then you ask him to play the salesperson's role while you offer objections. Analyze his performance.

In another case, you notice that Anne tends to do a lot of yes-butting: "Yes, the price looks a bit higher than what Gunrex has quoted you, but when you look at our liberal service arrangement and quantity discounts, you'll see that we are very much in line." Your advice is:

> I want you to start thinking in terms of yes-and. I'm going to run through some objections, and to each, I want you to figure out a way to say yes, and . . . instead of yes, but. . . . For example, when I talk about your price, you can say something such as, 'Yes, I can understand that that is a consideration, and here's something else you will want to consider.' Then sell another benefit.

You actually run through a drill, requiring her to think each time in terms of acceptance rather than the denial or rebuttal that yes-but implies. In any role-playing situation, you may find it necessary to run through it, give a critique, and run through it again.

It is quite difficult for some salespeople to keep silent after asking for an order. You can help them practice by having them act as the seller, close, and then sit. You, playing the prospect, remain silent for a long time, forcing the salesperson to do so as well. After a few times, the salesperson will be better able to handle the tension that builds during silence.

Making Calls Jointly

There's a certain etiquette that you'll want to observe when you plan to make sales and service calls with a salesperson. First and foremost, you must recognize that the territory belongs to the salesperson, even though it is in your district, region, or division. When you visit it, you are just a visitor. When you decide to make joint calls, remember that you want the salesperson to look good, the products or programs to appeal, and the company to be presented in the most favorable light possible. You also, to the extent possible, want the salesperson to feel good about your presence and working with you.

Before you go into a salesperson's territory, negotiate a good time. If he or she is in a critical stage of negotiating a key contract, this is not the time to introduce yourself into the process or to divert the salesperson's attention away from this final phase of the sales campaign. A manager who calls a salesperson up and announces "I plan to be in your territory next Tuesday and Wednesday'" could come across as uncaring and intrusive.

Let your salesperson know what you'd like to happen. If you plan to make calls, say so very clearly. If you have preferences about the kinds of calls you'd like to make, be up-front about that. For example, "I hope we can see a mix of old and new customers, if possible." Or, "I'd like to concentrate on new prospects." Or, "I think it would be helpful if we could make a couple of service calls," if you suspect that the salesperson is having problems in that area. If you don't specify that you'd like a mix of old and new, you may find that the salesperson has scheduled what we used to call a milk run—nice, safe customers who will help the salesperson make a favorable impression on you.

Be sure to give sufficient advance notice—a few days, at least—so that the salesperson can schedule calls with prospects and customers who will not be annoyed at the presence of a third party. Sometimes it's necessary for the salesperson to advise the prospect that someone else will be there. Most people don't mind if they're warned, but some prospects or customers may be so sensitive that it would be counterproductive for you to sit in.

What's Your Role?

Before a call, insist that the salesperson make it clear to you what role he or she wants you to play. At one end of the spectrum is the silent partner: You sit there and say and do nothing unless the salesperson calls upon you for specific action or information. At the other end, of course, is full and continuing participation in the sales process. You might even occasionally be asked to do the primary selling. As for the gray area in between, you want answers to the following questions:

> "Do you want me to speak up when I see the need or opportunity, or do you want me to wait for a signal from you?"
>
> "What kind of a signal should I expect from you?"
>
> "If I speak up, what are the constraints on what I say? Are there certain things I should be sure to include or to avoid?"

Without such a clear understanding, a manager can inadvertently create problems for the salesperson. I once made some sales calls with a fine salesman in Toronto. We hadn't discussed my role beforehand, so when a prospect brought up a matter that I had more knowledge of than the salesman, I jumped in with a lengthy explanation. After the visit, which produced no sale, the salesman said to me, tactfully, "I didn't want to get into that subject. I wanted to sidestep it." Oh boy.

Following are some rules of behavior that I have always found to be safe when I make calls with a salesperson. They generally don't create problems:

• *Don't take notes on a call.* The prospect will be distracted, wondering what you are writing down, possibly what the salesperson has done that's worng. The exception to this is when a prospect or a salesperson wants you to get back to him with some information or to follow up the call with some action on your part. Otherwise, sit quietly and try not to do anything that will divert the attention of either the prospect or the salesperson.

• *Never speak to a prospect or customer as "executive to executive."* You're there to enhance the salesperson's standing, if possible. You certainly don't want to make him or her look inferior to you and the prospect.

• *Try not to contradict a salesperson in front of a customer.* That's a sure way for the salesperson to lose credibility. And suddenly you risk thrusting yourself center stage. From that point on, the prospect will look at you to check that you agree with what the salesperson is saying. However, occasionally a salesperson might say something that could create a serious problem later. If the statement appears to be potentially dangerous, you might intervene as tactfully as possible. To illustrate: "Joan, there's been a change on that and I haven't had a chance to tell you. We're discontinuing that line effective the first of the month." Or, "What you just said has caused some confusion, and it was our fault in the home office. What we meant to say was. . . ." If you can take as much of the burden for the misstatement or misunderstanding on your own shoulders, you can minimize whatever damage your intervention may cause.

• *Don't correct a salesperson's selling mistakes.* This applies even though you think that the sale might be in jeopardy. There's always the possibility that what you view as a mistake is part of the salesperson's strategy. Any intervention might throw the salesperson off stride. It's better to turn the experience into a learning situation during the after-call analysis. Furthermore, you don't want to do anything to undermine the salesperson's prestige in the eyes of a customer. Your role is primarily as a partner and a resource, not as a rescuer.

• *Monitor your actions and words carefully.* Avoid creating the impression that you and the salesperson are ganging up on prospects. You don't want prospects to suspect that you are trying to overwhelm them or to catch them in a pincers tactic.

• *Let the salesperson handle objections.* Unless you have been asked in advance to help close the sale, respond to customer objections or stalls only if the salesperson clearly throws you the ball.

• *Volunteer no concessions to a prospect.* The salesperson may not want you to do it or may feel that when you do, you are under-cutting his or her credibility or impact.

• *Avoid piling on reasons to buy when a salesperson is trying to close.* Assume that if the salesperson wants help or backup from you, he or she will give you the signal.

• *Give the salesperson full credit for making the sale.* Even if you have been helpful in making the sale, do not detract from the salesperson's good feelings by claiming that you were essential to getting the action.

• *Never break the closing silence after a salesperson has asked for a prospect's agreement or commitment.* Sit still, say and do nothing to draw attention to yourself. (As a young salesman, I had a visiting manager break silence on a sale I was pretty sure I was about to get. He provided the prospect with just enough of a question that the sale was postponed, permanently as it turned out. I never wanted that manager in my territory again.)

Finally, when you return to the home office, write a note to the salesperson as quickly as possible, thanking him or her for the courtesy, and adding a note of encouragement. If you can find something to reinforce, this is a good time to do so.

Using Peer Mentors

Obviously you can't be everywhere. Consider supplementing your own field visits with those of other salespeople, from your region or outside. There are some clear advantages to using salespeople's peers for training. To begin with, the experience of having another salesperson looking over their shoulders may be slightly less threatening than having the boss do it. Another plus is that peers may actually have a bit more credibility than you, since they are still out there on the front lines, and you are not. A third benefit for both you and your salespeople in the field is that by using peers you can provide more frequent training. And don't overlook the valuable opportunity you present to the peer: learning how to train and be tolerant of other salespeople's approaches. If you are looking for a way to build a reservoir of management potential, this is a first-rate method.

There may also be some minuses to using peers for field visits. Many excellent salespeople are so highly competitive and ego-driven that they may not understand the virtue of helping other salespeople develop their own personal techniques in selling. Some of them may be too easily tempted to impose their own methodologies, which may be incompatible with the trainee's style and personality. I once visited the southern California sales region of the Research Institute of America (RIA), which was headed by a wonderful veteran salesman named Bob Montgomery. Most of the salespeople in the suite that morning complained about their lack of success in selling the concept of one of RIA's newsletters to supervisors who were enrolled by their bosses in an RIA self-development program. The difficulty surrounding this particular component of the program was that it was directed toward family and personal concerns, not matters of supervision. Prospects weren't sure they understood why they should be paying for such a publication. Bob, the manager, listened patiently to the complaints and then began to describe how he and another salesman had merchandised this particular report to a recent prospect. He told a verbal-proof story of another customer who had been thanked effusively by the wives of some of his supervisors for supplying them with valuable help in conducting family finances. And, of course, the customer—the boss—had felt appreciative and appreciated. Bob told the story in an old-fashioned way we called "romancing the product." It was warm, heartfelt, even a bit corny. It was also, to me, highly effective. But I knew that Bob had been unable to transfer that romancing skill to some of his salespeople. They simply approached selling too rationally. Perhaps their youth had a lot to do with it as well. The point is that Bob's verbal-proof story was like a foreign language to them. Bob did not try to impose his way of selling on his salespeople, but another and less sensitive person might have tried, with unfortunate results.

Another possible liability in asking certain salespeople to help you with other salespeople is that you are taking them out of selling for the moment. You can, of course, compensate them with a bonus for the time they are away from their territories.

A third potential problem is that people who sell well may not train well. Training takes patience, empathy, and the ability to listen and to articulate what needs to be done, again in the context of the salesperson's style and territory. As an example, two men on the home office sales staff had developed certain rather rigid approaches to selling some of the company's products. When they visited salespeople in the field, these two had the added clout of coming from the home office. When they trained, they conveyed the message, "This is the way to do this. There is no other." One man so threw me off stride in my territory with this unbending approach that my sales volume dipped for several weeks, and I informed my boss that I did not want to see that man in my territory again. A visiting peer can have an equally traumatic effect on a salesperson.

Finally, consider a salesperson's anxiety over what tales the mentor will carry back to the home office. A salesperson may have much more confidence in your empathy, even sympathy, than in an occasional trainer's discretion. As a salesman in the insurance business, I saw firsthand the damage that can be done by behind-the-scenes communicating by people who may be unqualified or insensitive. My sales manager had become enamored of the new trend in testing by psychological consulting firms, and many people in the sales force began to fancy themselves psychologists. A lot of the mail that went back and forth about salespeople was full of psychological references and amateurish analyses. Just before I left the company, I stumbled onto a file in my boss's office that contained some of this correspondence about me. Had I been planning to remain with the company, I doubt whether my career would have survived the nonsense.

Picking and Preparing Peer Trainers

In seeking out salespeople who are likely to be good candidates for training others, you should consider the following management functions, responsibilities, and potential liabilities that salespeople face when advancing into management. It's better to think about such matters before you decide rather than fret about them after.

- They'll have to be away from home.
- Their effectiveness as mentors will depend on the performance of others, rather than on their own.
- They may have to work with salespeople who cannot sell as well as they can.
- They may have to work with salespeople they don't like.
- They may have to accept selling methods that are very different from their own.
- They may have to be patient teachers.
- They may have to mute those qualities that make them superb salespeople.
- They may have to hear criticism of management policies and decisions that they have had nothing to do with, because they are seen as representatives of management.

Perhaps the single most important characteristic of good mentors is that they enjoy doing it. Good mentor/trainers receive gratification in helping others become even better, more effective, and more successful. They have a team or a group consciousness. Mentors like the idea of contributing not only to an individual's progress but to the upgrading of the group.

But most people, however intelligent and capable in their functions, are not natural teachers and coaches. People who are going out into the field to work with other salespeople should have some training themselves in how to train and coach. One sales manager I had employed peer mentors frequently. Unfortunately for those of us who depended on such training and guidance, some of these visitors were not terribly competent. They might have been great in their own territories, but they were not effective in helping the rest of us. In fact, I ran through three incompetent field trainers before I found one who was quite skilled. The ineptness of the field staff probably contributed to a turnover in salespeople that sometimes reached 100 percent in three months. And think of the skepticism that salespeople had when they heard they were about to be graced by the visit of someone whose competence they were unsure of.

Undoubtedly your training department can work with you in designing and delivering short courses in training and coaching that should be required for anyone working with others in the field. Otherwise, the damage can be considerable.

Controlling Peer Mentors in the Field

There is another somewhat delicate issue that should be anticipated. Now and then, you encounter a visiting mentor who, away from home, can get a bit wild. I have heard complaints of some visiting trainers drinking heavily, womanizing, and partying until all hours, rendering them not very useful the next day. In one company the problem got so bad that the peer mentors were called into a special meeting and warned that their behavior was offensive to many of the salespeople they visited—men and women who valued family life and responsibility. Remember that the image your mentors project has an impact on the morale and possibly even the motivation of your salespeople who have to work with them.

These days, when many of our best salespeople are women, a discussion of sexual harassment is a prerequisite for any field assignment. Peer mentors have power, no question about it. They can easily suggest that their word in home office ears can enhance or impede a career. Even if he is not a designing man, we have to face reality. He is working with a woman, possibly young and quite attractive. He spends hours with her, making calls, sharing meals, maybe even socializing briefly after the workday is over. It's not unnatural for a man to be turned on considerably by a pretty, skilled, and charming woman, and possibly to misinterpret her friendliness and rapport as an invitation to cross over the line. With such a misguided trainer, you risk not only losing a good saleswoman but a lawsuit as well. Of course, the mentor may have no sinister or manipulative intentions. Two people working together, perhaps socializing a bit as well, can develop a friendly and respectful relationship. The mentor must take special care in such a situation not to be seen as taking advantage of the relationship to become sexual, even in words only. If the mentor does *not* maintain a strictly professional distance, at the very least you could have an embarrassed salesperson (as well as trainer) and at the most a salesperson who considers a more drastic stance, such as resigning or litigating.

In reality, whether the mentor is male or female (males do complain of harassment, too), the word must be clear: He or she is there on a corporate assignment and should try to avoid any action or statement that could be misinterpreted as inappropriate.

Finally, for best results, I believe that there should be a clear understanding between the salesperson and the peer mentor that the latter will not carry tales back to the home office. Encourage your mentors to make the point up-front, and then be absolutely sure that the contract is honored. If the mentor has reason to believe that the salesperson has serious problems that demand immediate attention, and if the mentor is unable to provide the corrective help, you should be alerted to schedule a visit as soon as possible to find out for yourself what is going on. There should be no further communication about a salesperson's problems, mistakes, failures, or deficiencies between the mentor and you without the salesperson's knowledge and approval. When a salesperson worries about what a visiting mentor might be carrying back to the home office, that person is going to be guarded and nonrevealing.

Demonstrating

Whoever is making the visit—either a peer or you—should be prepared to take over calls occasionally to demonstrate certain points. After the call, encourage an analysis:

You: What did you hear me say when I asked for the order? Feed me the words as precisely as possible, Jan.

Jan: Let's see. You said something like, "There's the evidence that we can save you 18 percent a month from the outset. I know you'll want to start putting that 18 percent into your bank account as soon as possible. I can have this going for you in three days. Just give me your OK right here."

You: That was the first time. How about the second time I closed?

Jan: Uh, "This is the amount that you're spending needlessly every day. It comes to about $180. So, every day that we're not doing business with you, you pay a premium. Here's what I'm prepared to do. I have to call the home office to get approval, but I know I can do it. I'm going to set the effective date as of today, even though it takes at least three processing days. That way, you'll start saving almost $200 from right now. With your approval, I'll set this up just that way."

You: That's pretty good recall. Do you remember what you said on the last call, before this one.

Jan: Yes, I said something like, "Does this make sense to you?"

You: Then what happened?

Jan: Nothing. She thought for a long time and said, "Yes. **See me in** three months."

You: You see, you hadn't really closed. When you say things like that or, "What's your reaction to this?" you're really not asking for the order, you're asking for an opinion.

In another case, the manager or peer might demonstrate how to ask questions in sequence to get the prospect involved, or to answer questions: "Did you notice how I always paused before answering. It suggested I was thinking about the question, and that's flattering to the prospect." Or, "Run through for me what you heard me do when he interrupted the presentation to ask how much it costs."

Once I watched a top salesman demonstrate how he handled a visual. He turned the pages slowly and delicately, just as you would handle gold leaf. That was several years ago, and I still have vivid recall of the moment.

Following Up Your Visit

It's a good idea to follow up a visit to a salesperson's territory with an informal letter, reiterating the change or the improvement that the two of you agreed on. If you have any afterthoughts about how the salesperson can make the change more easily, completely, or quickly, the letter is a good place for them. If you can also summarize some of the things that the salesperson does well, or some of the competencies you observed, the letter becomes a reward, a reinforcement, and an encouragement. Send the letter as soon as you can, while the details of your visit are still fresh in the salesperson's mind.

If you telephone between visits, you might want to ask the salesperson how the action plan is working out. What have been the successes? What are the frustrations or disappointments? Such questions convey your continuing interest in the change being made and the message that you regard the action plan as important to you—quite the opposite of out of sight, out of mind.

Using Internal Rewards

If you refer back to the self-assessment on style at the beginning of this chapter, you'll find a number of statements that refer to the manager's role, even obligation, in helping salespeople actualize their potential for the long term. Specifically, statement 5: "I believe that I have an obligation to my salespeople to help them become as effective as possible and to fulfill their potential as sales professionals." Statement 9: "The long-term development of my salespeople is as high a priority as their short-term results." Statement 17: "Generally I believe that my salespeople are eager to achieve greater effectiveness in selling and to grow as professionals and people."

The continuing and lasting development of your salespeople's potential is unquestionably one of the objectives of your partnership role, as those statements attest. Now consider statement 2: "I believe that my salespeople bring to this partnership certain strengths, resources, knowledge, and experience that I must respect and that can be applied to building a more effective sales group." Interestingly, one of the resources that your people bring to the partnership are their drives toward the personal rewards they seek. I suspect that many managers don't think in such terms, but your salespeople's internal rewards provide you with powerful assistance in helping them become more effective in both the short and long term. Too many sales managers restrict their thinking to the external rewards they control—discussed in detail in Chapter 5—but the reality is that a manager can influence the power of the internal rewards, those that come from within the salesperson.

Internal rewards are probably even more forceful than external rewards in determining the commitment of salespeople to your objectives: You need to understand how to use them to enhance your persuasive power in the partnership. When you harness their internal rewards, you make the work much more meaningful and gratifying than it otherwise might be.

Kinds of Internal Rewards

Some of the internal rewards that salespeople seek and give themselves are:
- Growth
- Confidence in their competence
- Self-esteem
- A sense of achievement
- An awareness of social standing (among their peers)
- A feeling of belonging to the group
- Satisfaction in the work and achievement

They motivate your salespeople to excel, and you play an essential role in helping them identify these rewards.

Following are some statements that a manager might make to a salesperson. From the list of rewards above, select the rewards you believe the manager is trying to define and activate in each case.

I think you've having a problem with the kinds of objections you're getting. I suspect you don't like them. Who does? But I can see that with each call you're getting more confident in your ability to deal with them. One of these days you'll probably find that they can't throw much of anything at you that you can't field. And then you're going to feel so good about yourself and your selling.

*   *   *

When I look at the figures, they're wonderful. You took a territory that had been in the doldrums for years. And look, nine months later, you've upped the average volume over the past five years by almost 40 percent. So far as I can see, that curve is still going up. That's something to be proud of.

*   *   *

You know, your campaign to land this account was almost a textbook job of selling. If you can systematize what you did and make it work on other big accounts, you're going to see your volume jump. And I'd like to have you give a session at one of our meetings on landing the big account.

*   *   *

Your presentation is so much better organized than it was a few months ago. You really got my attention and kept it, even though I knew what you were going to say. And I think you'll be unstoppable if you could pare about ten minutes from it. Do you feel confident about doing that, now that you know the secret of organizing it?

*   *   *

What I hear from some of the others in the region is that you are willing to share your techniques with them. They say you are very generous.

*   *   *

I know that you're apprehensive about using the telephone more, but I also know that you're not the kind of person who will tolerate that kind of fear very long. You see it as a barrier to doing better, and I don't think you'll let it stay there.

*   *   *

If you suspect that you're one of the fastest developing salespeople I've ever had, you're absolutely correct.

*   *   *

Doesn't it give you tremendous satisfaction when you sit in an interview like the one we just went through and see yourself stay in there and close—well, I counted eight times? Remember when you said to me once how hard it was for you to close at all?

*   *   *

What I see in you is not only a good salesperson but a student of the selling profession. You not only know what to do, you're very aware of yourself throughout the whole process. I guess I'm trying to say that you process what you do while you're doing it.

*   *   *

"I realize that you want to go into marketing someday, but let me tell you how much I admire the way you are working to be proficient in every aspect of selling while you are a salesperson."

Many of the above statements are combinations of internal rewards. To elaborate, the internal rewards being activated by the statements, in order, are:

Growth, competence, self-esteem
Self-esteem, achievement
Achievement, social standing
Growth, competence
Social standing, belonging
Competence, self-esteem
Growth, self-esteem
Satisfaction, growth, competence
Competence
Competence, achievement

There are probably other internal drives and rewards in each statement. What is important about the above statements is that the managers uttering them are triggering motivators in their salespeople. Running throughout is the theme: You're good, and you can be better. When your salespeople respond to that kind of product, when they buy it from you, they go on to win, in most cases.

The most powerful appeals in selling relate to intangibles. You may sell a product, a program, or a service, but ultimately you open the prospect's eyes to some kind of emotional and psychological gratification. Let me illustrate by recalling a question from a workshop I recently did for loss-control specialists. These are representatives of casualty insurance companies that provide protection for the workplace. The specialists tour the plants, offices, and warehouses of policyholders to recommend steps the clients can take to reduce risk. One specialist, an engineer, suggested to a client that he could achieve greater safety by replacing a valve on a fuel storage tank. The businessman replied by saying that the valve in question had performed safely for years. Why should he incur unnecessary cost in replacing it with a more expensive valve? To the specialist, the client's question constituted an insuperable barrier. There was no way, the specialist said, to answer it logically. I advised that he answer it nonlogically. Here's how:

> Mr. Wright, in walking about and talking with your people, and in chatting with you, I'm impressed with the good relationships you have with your employees, and your concern for them. I realize that the valve has functioned fine, and there's always the possibility that it will continue to function for an indefinite time. But just suppose it doesn't. Suppose it fails, and there's a release of fuel. One or more of your people might get hurt. I know it would be a terrible thing for you to see employees carried out of here on stretchers. I also know that you've probably had an image of that. All I'm suggesting is that you buy some peace of mind, some security.

By the same token, what are you asking your salespeople to buy? More success in getting business, more volume, more money? Of course. But your product is ultimately something of greater importance. Most people like money, but on any survey of employees' priorities, you'll likely find money only fourth or fifth on the list. Most of us work for intangible benefits. The money, the volume, the number of accounts, are all means to an end. Some salespeople like the glory of being number one on the production lists. They enjoy being looked up to and envied by colleagues. Others take pride in knowing that their skills are a match for any prospect. You'll find some salespeople who like the way their minds work in creatively searching for solutions.

Don't overlook the power of power. Being a star performer brings prestige. It adds value and worth and privileges that others don't have. One of the very best salespeople I ever knew worked hard to stay at the top. He liked to know that every so often, when he called the company president to talk, often critically, about some aspect of the operation, the president would listen. When I worked in group insurance, a small branch of the large general agency to which I was attached insisted on almost total autonomy. The branch manager and his associates were top producers, and they felt that they had earned the right to run their office the way they wanted, without interference from the general agent.

When you want the commitment of your salespeople to ongoing improvement, remember that your product ultimately is an intangible.

Just as you don't want to emulate the mistakes of managers who ignore the potency of salespeople's internal rewards, you also don't want to go to the other extreme and short them on the external rewards you have at your disposal. A combination of rewards, coming from within and outside, goes far to ensure that you get the kinds of behavior you want in your salespeople and that the new, improved effectiveness is permanent.

KEY TO CHAPTER 4

In the management of salespeople's motivation, and in the reality of adult learning, feedback is essential. There are, in general, two kinds of feedback: positive and negative. Salespeople need both: negative to correct what they are doing that they shouldn't, and positive to encourage them to keep on doing what they should.

Most of my work with managers over the past ten years has convinced me that relatively few are comfortable giving feedback, especially the negative type. They worry about demotivating subordinates by using the wrong words. They are anxious to avoid arguments with the people they criticize. They even fear that, after giving criticism, they won't be liked. The unfortunate result of this worry and fear and anxiety is that they frequently don't criticize. Thus, they miss out on a rich opportunity to help their subordinates become more effective.

In this chapter, you'll review extensive recommendations about how to achieve the performance results that you and your salespeople are looking for. Start with assessing your current feedback practices—informal as well as formal—to see what parts of the chapter you should pay special attention to.

Assessing Your Feedback Practices

Following are statements that reflect common feedback attitudes and practices by managers. With how many do you agree? Disagree? Compare your answers with the analysis that follows the assessment.

	Agree	Disagree
1. Most salespeople don't want to hear criticism of their performance.	_____	_____
2. Criticizing a salesperson is risky because you should try to stay positive with your salespeople.	_____	_____
3. When you do have to criticize, it's best to wait until you have a number of things to say all at once, otherwise the salesperson will regard you as carping all the time.	_____	_____

	Agree	*Disagree*

4. There's bound to be a certain demotivation in salespeople who have been criticized for their performance. _____ _____

5. You're not going to be able to get improved performance from salespeople whose work attitudes are poor until you convince them that their attitudes must improve. _____ _____

6. When you're criticizing a star performer, you need to be tactful and diplomatic, because high producers are usually temperamental and proud. _____ _____

7. When you have to give serious negative feedback, it's best to try to have something positive to say as well, so the salesperson isn't demoralized and will be more accepting of the criticism. _____ _____

8. When a salesperson resists being criticized, have a list of other performance problems from the past ready to convince the salesperson of the seriousness of your feedback. _____ _____

9. Criticism should be delivered in private— always. _____ _____

10. When you hear a bad report on a salesperson from a customer or another salesperson, you shouldn't criticize until you have heard the salesperson's side. _____ _____

11. With a salesperson who is a good performer, it's not necessary to give detailed criticism. Just a brief mention of the problem will do. _____ _____

12. Don't encourage the criticized person to explain or excuse the failing or mistake, because any such explanation is usually self-serving and a waste of time. _____ _____

13. Since periodic performance appraisals cause stress in salespeople, it's better if you don't tell them in advance that the discussion will be a performance evaluation. _____ _____

	Agree	*Disagree*
14. It's better to give everyone an average rating on evaluations rather than risk discriminating against anyone.	_____	_____
15. Appraisals are a headache, and it's usually better not to make a big deal of them, so as not to upset good salespeople.	_____	_____
16. It's better to err on the side of strictness in appraisals than on the side of leniency.	_____	_____
17. You can soften the tension related to an appraisal by talking about the reward—a raise in base salary or a bonus.	_____	_____
18. If a good salesperson objects to any part of an evaluation, it's better to change the rating rather than create resentment in the salesperson. A salesperson's goodwill is more important than what higher management thinks about the appraisal.	_____	_____
19. If there is an argument about a rating, the manager's view must prevail.	_____	_____
20. The appraisal interview is a good time to make sure that the salesperson has accurate feedback about his or her performance during the year.	_____	_____

These questions are presented to demonstrate why so many managers don't like to give feedback, whether it's in the form of on-the-spot criticism or appraisals. If they hold biases such as some of the above, then they can't do a very good job giving feedback. If the feedback doesn't work, then these managers are justified in disliking this particular managerial responsibility.

Analysis

Use the following analysis of the assessment checklist to determine which of your attitudes about feedback need to be adjusted.

1. **Disagree.** Most salespeople welcome criticism if they believe it will help them be more effective in their selling.

2. **Disagree.** It is a myth that salespeople are so fragile and easily discouraged that you must not be negative with them. In reality, most

successful salespeople are discerning, balanced people. I can sense when a positive cover is being used to mask something unpleasant.

3. **Disagree.** Such laundry lists are inexcusable. If you have something to say to the salesperson, say it right away. Don't let matters pile up just to have an impressive load. Laundry lists overwhelm people and discourage them. They also feel resentment about being beaten down.

4. **Disagree.** Actually, constructive criticism usually contributes to motivation, because it points the way to achievement and success. Of course, if criticism is given poorly or destructively, the salesperson may well experience a decline in enthusiasm, commitment, and motivation.

5. **Disagree.** You shouldn't try to improve attitudes. You wouldn't know whether you were successful in doing so, because you can't see an attitude. But you can see behavior, and you can work to help a salesperson change behavior. Maybe attitude will change with it. Who knows?

6. **Disagree.** I agree with the adjectives temperamental and proud. Many star performers are. But usually they are also fanatic about shining even more brightly. If a manager's negative feedback shows them what is preventing them from doing that, they'll accept it.

7. **Disagree.** This is another common myth. As you'll see later in this chapter, mixing positive and negative often results in the salesperson's getting mixed and unclear messages. Keep your criticism clean and clear.

8. **Disagree.** For the same reasons expressed in the answer to number 3.

9. **Agree, absolutely.** You want to change behavior, not cause the salesperson to hate you for causing public humiliation.

10. **Disagree.** Don't criticize at all based on hearsay. There's too much room for argument. If you get a bad report and believe that someone should know about it, say to the salesperson, "I want to pass along some information that came to me, because it disparages you, and I think you ought to know it's out there." If the salesperson wants to explain, fine. But don't press it. The message has been delivered.

11. **Disagree.** Criticism should be specific so that the salesperson has no question about what should be done to correct the problem. Besides, a brief mention may disguise how seriously you take the deficiency. Don't suggest that the matter is minor when you regard it as sufficiently major to bring it up.

12. **Disagree.** It may be self-serving, but it may also be something you should know about the salesperson, your management, or the company's policies and procedures. It only takes a bit of time to listen. You don't have to agree with what the salesperson says, just accept that the salesperson may believe it.

13. **Disagree.** Salespeople ought to have time to think about what is to be evaluated. And if they have had feedback throughout the year from you, they should know what to expect. Of course, if their performance is poor, there will be stress whether there is advance notice or not.

14. **Disagree.** When you average your ratings, you probably discriminate against everyone. Averages are inevitably unfair to some and misleading to others.

15. **Disagree.** Appraisals are supposed to be a big deal, since they are intended to help salespeople get better at what they do.

16. **Disagree.** How does excessive strictness serve the process any better than excessive leniency?

17. **Disagree.** If a salesperson knows there will be a reward, he or she will sit there in anticipation and may not hear the performance matters that you want understood.

18. **Disagree.** This practice will surely make a joke out of the evaluation process. You should be prepared to explain the basis for an evaluation, and you should also be prepared to change it if there are extenuating circumstances that justify a change. But if you are convinced of the reasonableness of your appraisal, stick with it.

19. **Disagree.** For the reasons expressed in the previous answer. A salesperson may present justification that alters your view.

20. **Disagree.** Does that surprise you? A salesperson should receive accurate feedback all year. There shouldn't be any surprises at the evaluation.

4

Giving Critical Feedback That Motivates

People need to know how they are doing. Feedback on performance is essential to learning and improving. Of course, no one likes to hear about their mistakes and deficiencies, but that doesn't mean they won't welcome criticism if they can see the benefit of acting on it. Most working people want to be effective, to get the results they want from their efforts, and salespeople as a group are probably more concerned with their effectiveness than other categories of employees, especially those salespeople on incentive compensation.

Feedback can range from the impromptu curbstone variety after a sales call to a more serious discussion about a substantial problem to the penultimate counseling session for a major performance problem that could lead to termination.

In these pages I often equate feedback with criticism, but that can be misleading. Positive feedback actually constitutes a reward for good selling, which is dealt with in the next chapter. Such positive reinforcement is usually much more effective than negative feedback, if only because the reinforcement of effective behavior encourages its repetition. Criticism generally concerns itself with deficiencies that should be stopped or corrected. It doesn't take a psychologist to realize that doing something and getting rewarded for it is infinitely more attractive and powerful than being told to fix something that's wrong.

Mixing Positive and Negative

Ideally, praise and criticism should be kept separate, to keep the respective messages clear, clean, and free of any suspicion of manipulation. But things are seldom ideal. There are times when you must deliver the whole message at once, the bad with the good. For example, you have limited time with a salesperson, and you don't have two separate occasions on which to give feedback. Or a salesperson is working on a special project, and you need to give a progress report. If you follow the recommendations below, you can hope to deliver positive and negative feedback without seriously confusing the two or lessening their impact:

1. *Start with the negative.* That way, your salespeople won't worry that you're trying to soften them up. And if you start with the positive and they anticipate that criticism will follow, they will be so distracted that they won't hear the genuinely good things you have to say. You might say, "I have some positive things to say to you, but let's get the minuses out of the way first." Cover what is wrong without praising.

2. *Get agreement on the points of your criticism.* You may both prefer to get on to the good stuff, but there's no point in giving criticism unless the salesperson on the receiving end agrees with your negative points. You have to be sure you have that agreement before you can be confident that corrective action will be taken.

3. *Agree on remedial action, if required.* What will the solutions or alternatives be? Agreement is one thing, but a firm action plan is needed as well.

4. *Keep positives and negatives in proportion.* Resist the urge to exaggerate some of the good features of the salesperson's work to ease the pain of the negative aspects you have just unloaded. Keep the positive message in proportion to the negative. Here's an illustration of feedback in which the negative message is weightier than the positive:

Dave: Al, I'll be candid. There are pluses and minuses, and I want to cover both. First, what's wrong. You had to know from the copy of the shipping order that the quantities were wrong, yet you didn't warn the customer. According to Talbott, he didn't hear from you until he had already discovered the error. But you told me that yourself. I don't know why you didn't take fast action when the error was first apparent, but you didn't. We very nearly lost a customer. And we incurred considerable expense in rushing a replacement shipment to him. That's very serious stuff in my view. What do you say?

Al: I agree, Dave.

Dave: OK. In the future, I want you to agree to examine every copy of every shipping order the day it reaches you. No exceptions. Right?

Al: Right.

Dave: I also have a small pat on the back for you. It does not balance your goof, but I can say that once Talbott yelled, you moved fast. You arranged the special shipment from the home office in good time.

That's pretty straightforward. Al can't very easily miss the unspoken message: You did well in cleaning up a mess you shouldn't have made in the first place. Now here is a case in which the opposite is true—the good outweighs the bad:

Sheila, there's a pattern in your callbacks that I've noticed, and you need to know what I see. In the three callbacks we made, you weren't prepared with a good opening statement that explained why you were there. No matter how small a benefit statement is, it's better than simply showing up. Say that you've received new information, that you've thought about something he said last time that suggests another solution, whatever, but give a reason for making the callback. That's the negative. Do you understand what I'm saying? Good. Now let me give you a solid compliment. Once you had the chance, you sold hard. You weren't going to be a push-over. I like the way you stay in there until the prospect stops the interview. Persistence like that is very commendable. On balance, I'd say that what you did well far overshadows what you need to work on.

5. *Don't return to a discussion of the negative, if you can help it.* You have already established an understanding of what is wrong and needs to be fixed. Leave it for now. You don't want to take the pleasure out of the praise.

The Sandwich Technique

It's understandable when a manager wants to reduce the pain and embarrassment that accompanies giving criticism. To lessen the tension, some managers like to add a positive word to the negative. For example, "I almost hesitate to mention this item, because generally you're very scrupulous in keeping your activity up, but I can't help noticing that your daily average number of presentations has dipped about 20 percent in the past two weeks." Most of us would consider a 20 percent drop a serious matter, suggesting an ongoing problem rather than simply a momentary and soon-to-be-corrected slump. But this manager risks trivializing the drop. He approaches it timidly, reminding the salesperson that she has been a good and faithful employee. The manager regrets having to mention it; he has no choice but to bring up this unpleasant subject.

Unfortunately, backing into criticism deprives it of impact. In the above statement, the negative observation is almost buried. First the pat on the back, and then a slight jab to the chin. You can hardly blame the saleswoman for dismissing the feedback as not very important. Her response might well be, "Don't worry. It'll be up next week." You can almost hear the manager breathe a sigh of relief as he turns to more pleasant matters.

In other situations, managers explain their mix of positive and negative messages as helping to relax their salespeople and make them more accepting of the criticism—the sugarcoat-the-pill approach. Nowhere is this approach more evident than in the sandwich technique of criticism. Here is a manager who wants to remind her salesperson that he caves in too easily:

> You know, Pete, I was sitting there in the corner watching you give that masterful presentation that I've come to expect from you. You have such an easy, friendly style. He couldn't help but be carried right along. I think you probably give one of the smoothest, most interesting presentations I have ever heard. You might want to make everything perfect by sequencing a couple of more closes. I was a bit surprised to see you fold after one close. He did sound rather convincing when he told you he would be prepared to make a decision

on this next week. Of course, knowing you, I thought perhaps you were in control of the situation, that you knew something that I didn't. You see, that's how much confidence I have in you. You deserve it, with your record.

That's pretty impressive. Pete probably felt good about what he'd heard—at first anyway. Then, as he thought some more about it, he might have begun to wonder about what she had done to him. The sandwich technique, widely used, smacks of manipulation. "I'm thinking one way," the manager suggests, "but I want you to believe I'm thinking another way." The praise dilutes the criticism; the criticism contaminates the praise. The short-term effect may be pleasant and disarming; the long-term results will often be resentment and a possible loss of trust in the manager.

Curbstone Coaching

One of the best and most frequent opportunities to give salespeople feedback is through what has traditionally been called curbstone coaching or, more accurately, curbstone feedback. This is usually done in those few minutes immediately following a sales call, when what happened, or didn't happen, is still fresh in your minds. One obvious value of the curbstone feedback session is that the salesperson's behavior can be modified or corrected on the very next call.

By setting aside a few minutes after the call to analyze what went on and discuss what could be improved—either over coffee or driving to the next appointment—you can achieve an almost instant payoff on your advice. Of course, you need to make sure that the feedback is presented in a way that's truly helpful and acceptable to the salesperson. Here's an example of curbstone feedback. Ty and his boss, Malcolm, have just emerged from an interview that hasn't gone well, and Ty asks his boss for comments:

> There were a number of things that got in your way. For example, do you realize how long your answers to the prospect's questions were? You went on and on several times, and

I think he stopped listening. Also there were a couple of times when I thought you had him. You could have tried for a close, but you seemed reluctant to do it. How come? And another thing; it's small, but it could matter. You moved your chair from in front of his desk around to the side without asking his permission. He didn't look too pleased. You need to be careful about that.

If you're thinking that Malcolm's feedback wasn't as helpful as it could have been, you're right. True, the response was specific, but the manager committed three obvious feedback errors. First, he rattled off a small laundry list of mistakes that could be too much for Ty to absorb in such a short time. Second, he negatively labeled Ty's behavior by suggesting that the salesman was reluctant to close. When giving feedback, you should merely describe behavior without getting into attitudes or possible motives behind it. "Why didn't you close on those two opportunities?" would have been more appropriate. Ty may not have recognized them as opportunities. Malcolm's third mistake is the most serious. Ty's tendency to give rambling answers indicates a problem that's too complicated to be corrected by a simple suggestion to give shorter ones next time. This kind of disorganized thinking calls for extended coaching or training.

In another example, Amy has just concluded an excellent presentation that led to a sale. Even so, she asks her boss, Cal, for his reactions and suggestions for improvement. His response: "Hey, you got the order. Whatever you did must have been right." Cal has just missed an opportunity to help Amy pinpoint the key to her success so that she'll be sure to repeat it on the next call. He should have said something like this: "I admire the way you went immediately from the presentation to the close. It was seamless. I don't know how conscious you are that you don't hesitate for even a split second, but you should continue to do that.

Cal may have assumed that Amy was aware of everything she did, and that assumption could be incorrect. But even if Amy did understand the things she did right, a little positive reinforcement would only help her feel that much better about herself.

Below are some more recommendations that will help you give effective impromptu feedback:

• *Give one criticism at a time.* Salespeople may get discouraged if they come away from every call with a list of their mistakes. "How can I hope to do a better job when I do so many things wrong?" they may silently ask themselves. To avoid this, pick the problem or flaw that you believe can be most easily corrected or is the most important of several. As illustrations:

> While the prospect was explaining his objection, you sat there with a smile on your face. That could signal condescension. When the prospect starts talking, concentrate on looking attentive without smiling.

> * * *

> You flipped the pages of the catalog. Treat those pages with respect. Don't be so casual.

> * * *

> When you put your visual in front of the prospect, you moved some papers on her desk without asking whether you could. Next time, be sure to get permission before you touch anything on the desk.

> * * *

> Sometimes you speak awfully fast. Be conscious of it. Slow down. Look at me occasionally. If I give a slight nod, it means that you're talking at about the right speed.

> * * *

> I know the objection was easy to answer, but you moved so quickly to answer it that the prospect might have thought you didn't respect his thinking. When that happens again, count to five before you answer.

• *Stick to behavior you can describe.* Be aware that when you get into attitudes or motives, you're entering swampy territory. Because you can't see these things, you can't measure them. A comment such as, "You seemed afraid to ask for the order," or "Don't be embarrassed when the prospect makes a joke," might lead to a defensive answer such as, "I wasn't afraid," or "I wasn't embarrassed." Obviously this kind of exchange is counterproductive, so why get bogged down? Instead, talk only about what the salesperson did or did not do. And whatever you do, don't label behavior. Don't say such things as, "You were boring" or "What you did was not very professional."

• *Postpone dealing with complex problems.* A salesperson who rambles on or argues with prospects, exhibits nervousness, or doesn't really know how to give an effective presentation needs more than just a simple curbstone chat. In such cases, you should set aside some time, perhaps at the end of the day, to have a more in-depth discussion. You may even decide that some formal training is indicated. Remember: If you try to correct major problems between calls, you may wind up discouraging or confusing the salesperson and adversely affecting subsequent calls.

• *Reinforce the effective behavior.* No matter how skilled the salesperson is, always find something to praise. It shows that you're attentive and that you value the salesperson. Some examples: "I really admire the way you kept your cool when the prospect started giving you such a hard time"; "You deserve a lot of credit for sticking with your presentation after the prospect began to insist he had another appointment"; "Your manner of asking questions is so smooth that it doesn't threaten anyone and you always get the information you want."

Conscientious, consistent, skilled curbstone coaching means that at the end of the day, you'll have a better, more effective, and usually more highly motivated salesperson than the one you started out with that morning.

Handling the Bigger Problems

The curbstone variety of feedback is a wonderful tool in the continuing improvement effort when the problems are minor and easily corrected. But what do you do when the problems are more complex? Following is a five-step sequence you can use in discussing more serious problems with your salespeople. When you follow it, you stay on a well-defined path and avoid the swampy shoulders that could entice you into arguments, anger, and frustration.

1. *Define the behavior that you don't want.* Be sure you stick to behavior—not attitudes or motives—and be careful to avoid making accusations you can't substantiate. For example:

> Paul, here are three contracts you've written, all with impossible installation and starting dates. I know that you know that we can't be up and running in under three weeks. Yet suddenly, for reasons I don't understand, you've departed from standard procedures and caused a lot of headaches for the home office people who have to explain what we can do and then try to pacify the customers when they get mad at us for not fulfilling your contract.

> *   *   *

> Sherry, your last two activity reports show some days in which you made no calls. You simply listed them as telephone days. I'm quite puzzled that you are setting such enormous periods of time aside for telephoning. I hope you remember that we've talked frequently about how I think that all of our salespeople should be out making calls on prospects at least part of every day. I don't believe that it's good to stay home a whole day just telephoning.

> *   *   *

> Mac, this is the second time that you've given discounts when the account doesn't justify it. The first time we backed you, even though you made the mistake. Now you've done it again, after we told you last time we wouldn't do it for you anymore.

> *   *   *

> Tom, your selling continues to be lopsided. You're concentrating on the X-17 and X-24 lines, and selling next to nothing on the D-5 and other lines. We expect our salespeople to sell across the board. You're compounding the problem: By confining yourself to the X lines, you're not calling on any large accounts, which would be more interested in the other lines.

In each of the above cases, the manager described the situation in terms of what the person did or did not do. He didn't suggest that Paul and Mac were trying to put one over on the company. He didn't accuse Sherry of goofing off. He could have implied that Tom was timid about approaching large prospects, but that would have been an interpretation that would undoubtedly have aroused defensiveness.

2. *Criticize as quickly as possible after the event.* If you object to the behavior or performance, you certainly don't want to see it continue, and neither should the salesperson if the performance deficiency is getting in the way of success. Describe the behavior while it is fresh in the salesperson's mind. For example, Sam's manager approaches him and says, "You know, Sam, I've been meaning to talk with you about some phone conversations you've had with customers that I couldn't help overhearing. Sometimes you have a tendency to be very brusque with people. Even I was offended, and I wasn't the target." Sam asks the manager to be specific, but the manager can't remember exactly what Sam said. Sam doesn't remember much about the incidents, so the feedback doesn't go anywhere. The only result is Sam's annoyance that his manager has hit him over the head without being clear about what he doesn't want Sam to do in the future.

There's another reason why you shouldn't delay criticism when it is warranted. A salesperson who's floundering knows that you're not happy about it. Waiting for you to say something can create anxiety. Or you may mistakenly assume that the salesperson knows how to correct the problem. As a young manager, I made such an assumption, but the problem didn't get any better. By the time I finally approached my subordinate about it, he said, "I've been wondering when you were going to say something." I had let much needless tension grow in both of us.

3. *Get the employee's agreement that the problem is real.* Whatever you have observed, bear in mind that your salesperson might see the situation differently. To illustrate, Tom, whose selling has been lopsided, may have concluded from your past comments that the primary measurement of sales success was volume. Tom might respond, "Hey, I'm way above my quota in dollars. I thought that's what you wanted." Now you'd better clarify that your standards of performance are a bit more complex than that.

Sometimes you'll encounter salespeople who can't understand what the fuss is all about. They just don't buy your standards. If your standards are reasonable and your goals are relevant to the company's prosperity, make it clear to questioning salespeople that the point is not open for debate.

4. *Listen to the employee's analysis of the situation.* Even invite the salesperson's perception of what is going on. You might discover some extenuating circumstances. For example, Mac is defensive. He claims that he had to extend a discount because a competitor was offering a big price break, and using the discount was the only way he could land the business. It may be a rationalization. The manager then asks, "Why didn't you ask me before you committed us?" Mac rather sheepishly confesses that he was pretty sure the manager would turn such a request down, but he figured that after the deed was done, the manager would be reluctant to cancel a fait accompli. Besides, Mac continues, he was convinced that in another six months the volume on this account would grow to justify the discount. You listen, but you remind Mac that his presumption was reprehensible.

Sometimes a salesperson being criticized will try to sidetrack you. It's an understandable self-protective stance. To illustrate, Sherry admits that her car has been unreliable. She had it repaired—she thought—only to have it break down again. Apparently, to have the car repaired right will involve a large expense that she can't afford at the moment. Sherry has a product she would like her manager to buy—her car problem—but he doesn't. His reply is, "I'm sorry about your car problem, but I have a problem too. I can't afford to have you working part time. I want my problem solved." Sherry may reply, "I'll try to get the car fixed as quickly as possible." Much to her disappointment, her manager says, "No, that's not good enough. I want you to be a full-time salesperson, starting right now." He won't be shaken by her appeals for sympathy. He doesn't buy Sherry's product.

5. *Emphasize that you want improvement.* Spell it out. This is what you expect the salesperson to do. Of course, if you have learned that the salesperson was not entirely to blame, that there were indeed external factors that contributed to the performance problem, you'll want to take care of those, if you can. But continue to insist on the change you want and have a right to expect.

Encouraging Self-Analysis

Terry, one of your experienced salespeople, has just finished a lengthy and involved campaign to land a major new account. During the period of intense selling, she coordinated the efforts of a number of company people, specialists in certain processes. There were a number of peer contacts, group presentations, and seemingly endless callbacks. But in the end, success. You want to give her feedback on a few minor missteps, because you recognize Terry as a compulsive perfectionist. She needs to learn how to do better; it's a motivating force in her. But the flaws in the campaign were minor and you are reluctant to make the feedback a big deal. And you certainly don't want to dampen her tremendous pride in the accomplishment. In such a case, you might encourage her to conduct her own critique. Some steps to follow:

1. *Ask her to rate her work.* "Terry, on a scale of one to a hundred, what kind of rating would you give yourself?" Terry replies, after thinking, that she would give herself ninety. That sounds reasonable to you.

2. *Ask her to describe what she did well.* Terry talks, with obvious satisfaction, about the schedules she set up for the peer contacts, the tours she made of the customer's plant, and the group presentation that she orchestrated.

3. *Encourage her to talk about what went wrong.* "What do you think might have kept you from reaching a hundred?" Again, after much thought, she admits that she spent too much time in the beginning with a person who was not a decision maker, because she had not qualified him properly. She went on to fault herself for not having made the effort in the early stages of the campaign to identify someone who was a major influence and to cultivate him. By the time she did reach him, she had much missionary work to do to overcome his biases in favor of a competitor. Terry also describes her irritation with a pompous individual during the group presentation and how she probably offended him with her directness and coolness.

4. *Add your analysis.* First, ask her whether she wants to hear your comments. Undoubtedly she does. Start with the negative

things you saw that she didn't mention. "In some of the letters and the one report you sent the customer's folks, I thought you got pretty wrapped up in the technology, and I'm not sure everyone who read them, or listened to your presentation, was on your level of understanding. You wowed them, unquestionably, but you might have caused a bit of resentment in anyone who didn't follow you and didn't want to admit it." Then reinforce her predominantly positive analyses and add your own. "I was especially impressed with how you handled Ed Wright from the home office. Ed is not the easiest person to work with. He doesn't have much tact, but he was a pussycat working with you. And he paid you a high compliment. He said he thought you were one of the most competent people we have ever fielded."

5. *Ask for a plan of improvement.* "If you were starting over on this account, how would you avoid those traps you set for yourself? What would you do differently?"

By asking for such a self-analysis, you are also paying Terry a compliment. You convey the message that not only is she a superb salesperson, but she also has an objective view of herself.

Keeping Criticism Private and Objective

Remember that a salesperson with faults is a good person, but perhaps a bad wizard. You want something the person does to be corrected, changed, added, or improved, but you don't want to destroy the person in the process. Despite the momentary embarrassment or resentment over the criticism, a salesperson should be able to continue to work with you in comfort. The following dos and don'ts can aid you in delivering criticism that motivates:

- *Do be private with your criticism.* It's unlikely that a salesperson will hear much of what you are saying if there are others around who might overhear.
- *Don't be punitive.* Your language and tone should never suggest that you are "out to get" a salesperson for not performing correctly.

- *Do be positive.* The purpose of your criticism is to help a salesperson work more effectively and happily in the future.
- *Don't be personal.* You are questioning an aspect of the employee's behavior, not personal value and worth.

Dealing With Stars

I'm about to contradict myself. I've advised against giving multiple feedback that could be interpreted as a laundry list as well as mixing positive and negative feedback. However, when you work with a highly skilled, very effective salesperson, you may be justified in ignoring my advice. In such cases, you'll often discover that your negative feedback is so slight that it hardly suffers when you reinforce positively as well.

A few years ago, I asked one of my company's best salespeople whether I could accompany her on some calls while I was in the area. All day as we worked, she impressed me enormously with her superior competence. At the end of the day, before I headed for the airport, we had a drink. She asked me what suggestions I had for improving her effectiveness. Then she took out a notebook and a pen to write my comments down. There was something about a minor incident when she fumbled in her briefcase for something and talked to it rather than the prospect—a slight distraction during her presentation. My remarks were all of that nature. But I closed by adding, "These are very small refinements. Overall, this was one of the most interesting and satisfying trips I've ever made with a salesperson" Then I confessed my admiration for the way she had held on during an interview with an executive who kept pleading that he had a meeting to attend. Time after time she accepted and proceeded to sell and close some more. It was a masterful performance.

I didn't have qualms about giving her a list of things, because they were all very small, or in mixing positives with negatives, because the pluses were overwhelming. Besides, she was in such command of her skills that nothing I said could have detracted from her self-confidence. She closed her notebook and surprised me by telling me how grateful she was that I had taken the time to offer my suggestions. What a professional! She told me how frustrated she had been with other managers in the company. She always asked them for their recommendations, as she had with me, but they never provided any. They simply indicated that she was doing a superb job and had nothing to add. She felt, she said, very cheated, and a bit resentful. I learned a great lesson that day. Always have something to contribute even to near perfectionists. They expect it. They deserve it. And what are you there for, if not that?

Assertiveness-Responsiveness

In the 1970s, assertiveness training became popular in this country. The value of such training is that it helps you identify your needs and wants and express them in a way that is acceptable to others. It is especially useful in expressing things that are not terribly pleasant. Assertive techniques, therefore, can be valuable aids in giving negative feedback. There are four steps in an assertive statement:

1. *You describe the situation as you see it.*

Gene, you and I agree that your annual renewal rate of accounts has to remain above 80 percent. But for the first nine months of this year, you haven't succeeded in reaching a higher average than 72 percent.

2. *You describe how you feel about what you see.*

I'm not happy with this. In fact, I'm quite disappointed that you haven't fulfilled our agreement.

3. *You describe the change you want.*

I want to see you raise the average to 85 percent for the last three months.

4. *You describe the reward for making the change.*

If you can do that, then I'll give you a satisfactory evaluation. Otherwise, I'll have to put you on probation.

That's a straightforward statement. But suppose that you are talking with Carla, who has proved herself in the past to be a fine salesperson. You might wish to be a bit more responsive as well as assertive:

> 1. You describe the situation as you see it and invite her to tell you her perception.

Carla, we have a number of complaints from your customers about your follow-up when their deliveries are late or are in error. And that's a real problem, since it's going to affect your repeat business. I know you're aware of the situation. Right?

Of course I am, Charlie. These people are calling me to blame me.

> 2. You describe your feelings and ask about the other person's.

Well, we're upset in the home office, and I guess you must be pretty concerned.

Absolutely.

Continuing the assertive-responsive approach, you modify step 3:

> 3. What is the change we both want?

OK, I want to solve this service problem, and I know you do as well. What can we do?

First of all, Charlie, you can do what you said you were going to do. I told you last month that I was having some problems with Rick at the warehouse. He keeps on telling me that the problem is in my paperwork, that my instructions aren't clear when I fax them in. But I can't get a straight answer from him as to what he wants from me. And he tells my customers that I'm causing the problem. That doesn't help anybody. I told you that I don't know what's going on between Rick and me, and you said you were going to sit down with him and try to iron this out. But I've seen no results.

Carla, I owe you an apology. I did schedule time with Rick, and then something came up and I couldn't meet with him. Then it slipped my mind. I'm sorry. I see I'm part of the problem. Let me call him now and let's talk, the three of us.

The reward for both Carla and Charlie (step 4) is pretty obvious. In general, with most of your salespeople, an assertive-responsive (A-R) approach to any problem will work quite well.

The A-R technique can be highly effective when you're confronted with an unfavorable situation but you're not sure what has brought it on. In the following example, Trish, a field manager, is puzzled by the loss of a major account in Brad's territory. She and Brad sit down for a chat.

Trish: When Rogat decided to take its business to Apex, that really devastated the region. I'm not sure what happened, which is why I thought perhaps we should talk. I'm under the impression that there were service problems, but beyond that, I'm unclear. I know I'm terribly upset, because they had been with us for eight or ten years. But I can guess that you're pretty upset yourself.

Brad: A bit. I have to tell you, Trish, that I'm also quite angry. I don't think this should have happened. I also suspect that I'm the donkey people want to pin the tail on.

By using the A-R approach, Trish has opened up the discussion and given Brad a clear signal that she is ready to listen. What she hears is that there have been some foul-ups in the home office that the service people there have done their best to cover up.

In addition to being useful in an uncertain situation or in seeking information, A-R can be effective when you have a salesperson who is unusually sensitive or defensive in critical feedback situations. To illustrate, Ron, the manager, hopes to give Tammy some necessary feedback without getting trapped in an emotional backlash.

Ron: What I'm seeing in your presentations fairly regularly is that you get easily flustered when the prospect asks technical questions. I'm pretty sure that you know the answers to most of them, but what I suspect, and mind you, I'm guessing, is that the minute the question comes up, you tense up. I could see some of that. Maybe you're not listening as well as you could. That happens to all of us when we get tense. A couple of your answers today were not appropriate for the questions asked. It must be pretty embarrassing when you go to all the trouble of framing a good answer and suddenly realize it's not on target. I know I would be upset if that happened to me. And by the way, it has, especially when I've jumped right in before I was sure I knew what information the prospect wanted. Am I speaking to your difficulty?

Tammy: Well, yes, Ron, I sometimes do that, but I think everyone has that problem from time to time. Just like you said, you've experienced it too. I don't think it's realistic to suggest that I have a serious problem from a couple of mistakes.

Ron: I'm not trying to suggest that you have a big problem. I guess I'm more interested in asking whether you realize what happened today.

Tammy: Yes, but I thought I recovered pretty well.

Ron: Again, I'm not trying to make a case here. Why don't we talk about what you can do to prevent that from happening again, giving the wrong response. I think that's more important, to discuss a solution rather than fixing on a problem. Don't you?

Tammy: I do. I'm always open to bettering my presentations.

Ron: Of course you are. OK, let's see what kind of a technique we can develop that can help you zero in every time.

What Ron can do with Tammy is to demonstrate a two-step procedure for more accurately identifying the problem or question: (1) count to three after the prospect has finished talking, so as not to step on the question, and (2) make it a routine to ask a question for clarification before launching into the answer. "Are you referring to the average shelf life of the thinner?"

The A-R mode of communicating is also useful when you are especially frustrated or exasperated. To illustrate, Glen has repeatedly cautioned Erwin about the latter's tendency to argue with prospects when they seem to question Erwin's statements.

Glen: Erwin, I have to be totally up-front about what I saw. Twice when the prospect expressed some skepticism about a point you made, you acted as if she were a bit stupid. I've told you, probably three or four times, that I don't believe that's the way to handle a question or an objection. My memory is that we've worked on this habit of yours lots of times. Am I correct, that we've had this conversation before, and am I correct that you argued with her today?

Erwin: Yeah, I guess I do have a tendency to answer that way. I didn't think I was arguing today, but maybe it looked like that. If it did, I can see how you might be upset. I just haven't gotten the hang of handling that kind of thing.

Now Glen can try again.

Humor and Sarcasm in Feedback

Humorous feedback, slightly barbed, can backfire.

Hey, you poured on the charm so much in there that I thought you were trying out for the Miss Congeniality award rather than aiming for the order.

*   *   *

You ought to think about cleaning out that briefcase once in a while. You probably have some manuals left over from the Civil War.

I'm leery of making a joke at anyone's expense. Humor is easily misinterpreted, so why take a chance? And it can offend. Not long ago, I won an award for my writing. A few days later, I went to a meeting at which I ran into another writer who is probably much better known than I am in the field. Our acquaintance went back years. We chatted amiably until a third person joined us to congratulate me on winning the honor. The other writer asked, "You won it?" I answered, "Yes, eat your heart out," and I laughed. He didn't. I had taken liberties that I shouldn't have. I assumed he was secure in his reputation, but I didn't know that for sure. I didn't know him well enough to be sure he would laugh with me. I learned a very important lesson: Be sure you know the person you're kidding with. Even then, cracking jokes, especially at the other's expense, can be risky.

I'm even more fearful of sarcasm in remarks to others. Sarcasm usually suggests aggressiveness, an attempt to embarrass, put down, humiliate. To illustrate:

- A manager has just sat through a mild, pressureless interview that resulted in no action: "Well, that was a nice tiptoe through the tulips."
- A salesperson has failed to follow a manager's repeated advice, and the boss says, "I guess next time I'll hit you over the head with a two-by-four to get your attention before I give you a tip."
- A manager has been trying to explain what she thinks a salesperson ought to do in a certain situation, but the salesperson doesn't seem to grasp what she is telling him: "All right," she says, "let me try it again. My plane doesn't leave until six. I have all day."

- To a salesman who fails to pick up on buying signals, his manager says, "Wake up and smell the coffee." Or, "Hello, anyone at home? You had him and you didn't take advantage of it."
- After a rather disastrous sales interview, a salesperson asks her manager for feedback, and he replies, "Let me put it this way. That was not your finest hour."

Sarcasm hurts. If salespeople feel resentment at your words, they aren't listening to and accepting your counsel.

If you want to use humor, tell a neutral joke, one that doesn't seem to be a covert message about the salesperson's performance on a call. Or joke about yourself. Self-deprecating humor is always welcome.

Ensuring That Criticism Corrects

Of course you'd like to avoid the pain of giving your salespeople negative feedback. That's only natural. And you'd like to bypass arguments and fruitless debate. Although you can't always avoid the pain and embarrassment, you can take steps to better assure yourself that the criticism will help the person become more effective. Follow the items in this criticism checklist the next time you give critical feedback to increase the chance that your criticism will do exactly what you want it to do: help the salesperson become more effective.

Criticism Checklist

☐ I criticized as soon as possible after the event or behavior.
☐ I criticized the salesperson in private.
☐ I stuck to describing the deficient behavior.
☐ I described the deficient behavior specifically.
☐ The behavior I criticized was what I had observed or heard.
☐ I avoided discussing attitudes or motives.
☐ I avoided discussing previous, unrelated problem behaviors.
☐ I avoided criticizing while angry.

☐ I did not repeat hearsay.
☐ I did not mix positive with negative feedback.
☐ I took time to make sure that the salesperson understood why I felt that the behavior was deficient.
☐ I listened carefully to the salesperson's analysis of the problem.
☐ When the discussion strayed, I reminded the salesperson of the change I wanted to see.
☐ I enlisted the salesperson's aid in looking for a more effective behavior or approach.
☐ If the problem was beyond the control of the salesperson, I made a note to develop a plan to improve conditions.
☐ I pointed out the consequences of continuing the undesired behavior.
☐ I accepted the salesperson's feelings.
☐ The salesperson and I agreed on an action plan for improvement.
☐ We agreed on a time frame for accomplishment of the change.
☐ I looked for something I could learn from the feedback session.

Performance Appraisals

Performance evaluations are at least annual events, and they may be done as often as quarterly. The appraisal interview provides a superb opportunity for giving feedback. It is also an occasion for a manager to reiterate standards and goals, to tell employees what they are expected to do. That's the initial step in the management of your salespeople's motivation, based on expectancy theory. There's no better time to accomplish this than during an appraisal interview.

Evaluation time is when you and the salesperson should be thinking about performance goals for the forthcoming period. Those goals might include action plans for improvement and professional growth. Managers often confess to having mixed feelings about performance appraisals. So, for that matter, do salespeople. How do you feel about appraisals as a managerial tool? How well do they work for you? The following self-assessment quiz can help you develop a profile of your attitudes toward evaluations and your effectiveness in using them.

Assessing Your Attitude Toward Performance Appraisals and Feedback

If you've been managing long, you've had experience appraising the performance of your salespeople. How do you feel about appraisals? What are the best ways to get the job done? Following is a brief quiz to test your attitudes and preferred approaches.

	Agree	Disagree
1. Most appraisals produce stress in me.	___	___
2. To reduce stress in employees, it is better to schedule interviews without notice.	___	___
3. When the appraisal is fairly negative, it is best to open the interview with some positive statement about the salesperson.	___	___
4. It's permissible to include remarks by others about the salesperson being appraised as long as you identify the source.	___	___
5. I believe that a salesperson's potential ability should be included in the evaluation even when the actual performance is inadequate.	___	___
6. It's important for a salesperson to understand the basis for my evaluations.	___	___
7. When a person gets emotional during the interview, it is advisable to terminate the session and reschedule it.	___	___
8. It is better to evaluate too strictly than too leniently.	___	___
9. I should never refer to past appraisals.	___	___
10. An appraisal should produce no surprises for the employee.	___	___
11. An appraisal must refer to a salesperson's attitudes, because they must be changed in order to change behavior.	___	___
12. Since rewards should be tied to performance, I discuss any increase in base compensation during the appraisal interview.	___	___
13. I am usually not interested in the reasons for substandard performance or mistakes, only the improvement.	___	___

	Agree	Disagree
14. An ideal appraisal is a dialogue that produces specific goals and action plans.	___	___
15. One way to control the length of the session is to schedule it just before lunch or before I leave the salesperson's territory.	___	___
16. The salesperson must understand that what counts during the appraisal is how I perceive any problem.	___	___
17. Before I begin an appraisal interview, I have an idea of what I think should happen as a result of the session.	___	___
18. Salespeople should be consulted as to the best time for the interview so that they will be free from distractions and will have the opportunity to prepare.	___	___
19. It can be useful to let employees speak fully about their perceptions of a problem—and feelings about it—before we start to work on a solution.	___	___
20. The proper length of time for an appraisal is however long it takes to arrive at action plans that satisfy us both.	___	___

Analysis

1. **Agree.** This is the more usual answer. People generally don't like to have to sit in judgment of others, especially when they have to give negative feedback.

2. **Disagree.** There's bound to be stress if the evaluation isn't altogether favorable. At least let the salesperson come prepared to be a partner in the process and to help you conduct a constructive interview.

3. **Disagree.** If a salesperson expects some negative feedback, he or she isn't going to be attentive to your positive comments, especially if the salesperson suspects that your positive preface is a softening-up tactic.

4. **Disagree.** You may get into an argument over the source's credibility or understanding of a situation.

5. **Disagree.** Actual observed performance is the appropriate

matter for the evaluation. If you want to take potential into consideration, do so in setting goals and quotas for the coming period, preferably with the help of the salesperson.

6. **Agree.** The more data you can supply to support your evaluation, the more credible you are and the more authoritative the rating is.

7. **Disagree.** You have to expect some emotional reaction if the evaluation is negative. Accept that reality and the person's feelings, then move on. If the reaction is abusive or prolonged and the person is out of control, you don't have to tolerate the excess or insults. Say, "We can't continue under these conditions. When you're confident that you can work with me in a helpful way, we'll reschedule."

8. **Disagree.** If a salesperson believes that your appraisals are skewed in one direction or another, you could lose your credibility.

9. **Agree.** A salesperson shouldn't feel hounded by past deficiencies that have been corrected. And if they haven't, then you are well-advised to resolve them through counseling. If the problems are serious, they should not be permitted to persist.

10. **Agree.** If you've been giving salespeople feedback on their performance all along, they ought to have a good idea of how you're going to evaluate the overall period.

11. **Disagree.** You can't see or measure attitudes. Stick with changing behavior, and if the change is successful and rewarded, the attitude may change. But you probably won't know.

12. **Disagree.** If salespeople expect you to talk about rewards during appraisal interviews, they may not listen to what you think is important. So make it a policy: appraisal now, rewards some other time.

13. **Disagree.** You might learn something about your operation, the company, or support people that you didn't know. Be prepared to listen for any problem that needs your attention, but concentrate mostly on future behavior in the salesperson.

14. **Agree.** Your subordinate should be a partner in the process.

15. **Disagree.** Be prepared to take as long as necessary to do the job right.

16. **Disagree.** How can you make progress when a salesperson perceives a problem differently, or as not a problem?

17. **Agree.** But you should be open to modification if the salesperson makes significant contributions during the session.

18. **Agree.** If they're distracted or caught unprepared, they can't help you have a good evaluation session.

19. **Agree.** Let salespeople talk about how they perceive any difficulty. You need to forge a common base for a solution, and in some cases, you may have to change your perception of the situation when the employee's view makes more sense.

20. **Agree.** This is also the answer to statement 15.

The Purpose of Appraisals

When it comes to the subject of performance appraisals, managers and salespeople often have the same reaction: dislike and discomfort. Many managers complain that they are thrust into the role of "graders" of their people, and their salespeople often grumble that the evaluations are arbitrary, prejudicial, and distorted. The perceptions of both are grounded in reality. More frequently than not, the fault lies with the appraisal form itself, which may force people into playing parts they'd rather not. Some forms actually use a grading or rating scale with numbers, while others have sections that call for purely subjective responses by appraisers. But some of the bias against the appraisal function may also stem from a misunderstanding of the purpose of evaluations.

Don't think of yourself as sitting in judgment or as a teacher handing out grades; think of yourself as an enhancer and a resource. Through the appraisal, you are providing support and direction to your salespeople. When you project that kind of image, you'll be pleasantly surprised to find that your salespeople welcome periodic appraisals that provide feedback, measure their achievement, and map out the future. Such evaluations, even when they are critical, are essential to motivate your salespeople, who want to know how they're doing, what they should stop doing, and what they need to do better. The appraisal is an important time when managers and subordinates can come together and talk about how to improve performance.

There's an added benefit for you in the appraisal process: It can be a learning experience. By listening well and exercising patience, you can get feedback from your salespeople about your style of managing and its impact. You might also hear about company or your regional policies and procedures that could be inhibiting productivity.

When appraisals do what they're supposed to, wonderful things can happen. For example:

• *They form a contract between you and the salesperson.* Both of you agree on the goals to be accomplished and the performance standards you expect during the next period. Too many managers assume that their subordinates know what they want done. A good appraisal leaves nothing to chance. And don't forget: People need goals. There's no human behavior without them. A good goal that your salespeople buy into has motivational value.

• *Appraisals provide you with control.* You can plan and measure progress. You know when deviations occur in time and to step in and make corrections in your plans and goals.

• *They help you determine training needs.* You might discover that your whole sales force needs some refresher training in product knowledge or selling skills. Or you might conclude that some of your salespeople need more intensive coaching.

• *Evaluations help you spot salespeople with management potential.* Through performance reviews, you can spot the high potentials, the people who have both the will and the ability to go further in the organization.

• *Appraisals ensure that everyone is working in the same direction.* During the interview, you can convey the mission and goals of the organization to all your salespeople. You can also let them know that individual performance will be judged by its contribution to those goals.

Conducting a Successful Appraisal Interview

What makes a good appraisal interview? The recommendations below characterize a positive, helpful interview:

• *Give advance notice.* Your salespeople will appreciate having some time to think about the last year and make notes about their successes and mistakes. Prepared salespeople may have a number of things to tell you about their needs, your management, company operations, or barriers to effectiveness.

• *Present documentation.* The more facts, dates, and records you have, the more acceptable your feedback will be. And you won't open yourself up to the charge that your judgment is arbitrary or subjective.

• *Stick to observed behavior.* Evaluate only what you've seen and heard. Don't discuss hearsay; it's subject to misinterpretation. Don't get into attitudes.

• *Emphasize goals and outputs.* Achievement and productivity count. The inputs and means are less important. It may impress you that a salesperson has great enthusiasm, but how does that translate into sales? The same can be said for the virtue of cooperativeness.

• *Listen to your salespeople.* Successful evaluations are dialogues and partnerships. Salespeople have important stakes in their appraisals—their careers. Your subordinates could be giving you vital information about future assignments and development.

• *Control the interview.* You know where you want the interview to go, what results you want to achieve. Without dominating or censoring your subordinate, keep the session on track. Control in this situation means guiding, not pushing.

• *Discuss evidence available to both of you.* Ideally, there should be no surprises for the salesperson. If you've given feedback during the year, and if your evaluation criteria are known, then the salesperson will walk into the session with a fairly good grasp of what will happen. Many employees complain that the annual appraisal is the time when the manager springs unpleasant surprises on them. That's seriously demoralizing, demotivating, and debilitating for the manager-subordinate relationship.

• *Give specific feedback.* Statements such as "You're doing a good job" or "You'd better shape up" are almost without value unless they are accompanied by a specific description of what the salesperson is to continue or stop doing. If you have to deal with characteristics on the appraisal form, such as "positive attitude" or "shows initiative," show how those are manifested in what the salesperson does.

• *Make sure the salesperson understands problems.* When there is a performance deficiency, make sure the salesperson understands what it is and why it's a problem. Often it's an issue of making sure that your criteria and standards are clear. If you feel that they are reasonable, don't get into an argument about their fairness. You have a right to insist that your salespeople observe your standards and work to achieve your goals. If a particular salesperson is unable to do so, then you have a serious problem that may have to be dealt with through counseling or eventual termination.

• *Get a commitment to change.* Don't conclude the session with vague assurances. If there is a performance deficiency, get agreement on a plan to improve. What's to be done, how, and in what time frame?

• *Take sufficient time.* The interview should take as long as you believe is necessary for both of you to say what needs to be said and to achieve the necessary understanding about what has gone on and what will go on in the next period.

• *Accept the salesperson's feelings.* The salesperson may show signs of stress, anger, or disagreement. You don't have to agree with the feelings; just accept them and move on. Don't deny or disparage them, however.

The primary purpose of a performance appraisal should be to help the salesperson become more effective, to get more of the results that you and the salesperson want. Before your next appraisal session, check your own evaluation practices against the following checklist.

Appraisal Checklist

☐ As much time as necessary is set aside to complete evaluations.
☐ The evaluation system is presented positively as a means to help salespeople become more effective.

☐ Good evaluations lead to some kind of reward.
☐ The evaluation process takes place at least once a year.
☐ Appraisals confine themselves to work-related criteria.
☐ Appraisal forms are simple and easy to use.
☐ The appraisal criteria are applied uniformly to all salespeople in a given group.
☐ Questions or criteria are validated by actual performance results or activities.
☐ Questions concern themselves with behaviors and job functions.
☐ The appraisal form requires an explanation for the evaluation given.
☐ The salesperson to be appraised is given ample notice of the interview so as to be able to collect data and records.
☐ The appraiser holds the interview without interruptions.
☐ The salesperson's perception of the quality and quantity of the work done is part of the interview.
☐ Appraiser and salesperson develop an action plan jointly for the next period.
☐ The salesperson signs the form.
☐ Discussions of rewards for good performance take place separately.
☐ All objectives that have not been met are accounted for and explained.

Counseling a Salesperson With a
Serious Performance Problem

A failing or floundering salesperson who cannot or will not perform according to your standards should be given every reasonable opportunity to improve to at least a minimally acceptable level. But you have to determine what the word *reasonable* implies. Certainly you have an obligation not to abandon someone to failure if salvage is possible. On the other hand, you can't afford to have a persistent failure on your sales team. It's not fair to the company or to the other salespeople who report to you. And the sinking salesperson doesn't reflect well on you. At the same time, you can't permit a salesperson at the bottom to draw you away from your obligations to your other salespeople, who also need your attention and your help. The payoff on your investment of time and energy in good performers is far greater than you can usually hope for with a flounderer.

Face it: You may have to take drastic action with a salesperson who can't cut it. But before you do, you're well-advised to schedule a counseling session with the failing member of your team. It will help reassure you that you have indeed taken reasonable steps to save the poor performer. It will also help you should the salesperson later accuse you of discriminatory practices or wrongful discharge.

What's your perspective on counseling practices? The following self-assessment will give you a clue.

Your Counseling IQ

How confident are you in your skills in counseling a salesperson who has a serious performance problem, one that may lead to termination? Here's a self-assessment of your counseling know-how:

	Yes	No	Not Sure
1. Counseling is needed when a performance problem threatens to seriously disrupt a salesperson's productivity or that of the sales team.	_____	_____	_____
2. Salespeople who sense that they are incompetent or unproductive usually accept counseling.	_____	_____	_____
3. It's important to approach counseling with the attitude that the salesperson is not on trial, but his or her performance is.	_____	_____	_____
4. Performance appraisal time is usually the best time for counseling.	_____	_____	_____
5. When a salesperson is failing or not performing to requirement, you have an obligation to take every reasonable step to help the person.	_____	_____	_____
6. When you counsel a failing salesperson, you reassure others that you would help them overcome performance problems.	_____	_____	_____

	Yes	No	Not Sure
7. Salespeople who fail consistently should be quickly dismissed, or they will demotivate and demoralize others.	___	___	___
8. Salespeople who perform deficiently may not know what they are supposed to do or how to do it.	___	___	___
9. The more documentation of performance problems you have, the less stress you'll feel when counseling.	___	___	___
10. You should never counsel when you feel angry with the salesperson.	___	___	___
11. A healthy, sincere salesperson does not have negative feelings about counseling.	___	___	___
12. It is helpful if, during the interview, you can identify employee attitudes that contribute to poor performance.	___	___	___
13. It is helpful for you to listen to the salesperson's reactions even though you don't agree with everything said.	___	___	___
14. When the salesperson doesn't volunteer information you need, you should be patient and not forceful in your approach.	___	___	___
15. If you don't learn something about the salesperson, the operation, and the working conditions in the counseling interview, it is possible that the interview has not been a complete success.	___	___	___
16. When a salesperson's performance deficiency is caused by personal problems, you should try to understand what the problems are before you counsel.	___	___	___

	Yes	No	Not Sure
17. A good counselor encourages an employee to come up with a solution that he or she feels responsible to carry out.	⎯⎯	⎯⎯	⎯⎯
18. A successful counseling session is one in which you and the salesperson agree on a solution.	⎯⎯	⎯⎯	⎯⎯
19. It is a good idea to invite your own manager to the session to impress the salesperson with the seriousness of the problem.	⎯⎯	⎯⎯	⎯⎯
20. When more than one performance problem is involved, you should pick the one that is most serious, that has the highest priority.	⎯⎯	⎯⎯	⎯⎯

Analysis

1. **Yes.**
2. **Yes.** Most employees don't like to work ineffectively or to fumble, and they'd like to know how to do better.
3. **Yes.**
4. **Not sure.** Counsel at the performance appraisal only if the seriousness of the problem becomes clear at that time. Otherwise, schedule the session whenever the problem does become apparent. Don't wait for appraisal time.
5. **Yes.** You have an obligation to both the employee and your company, which has already invested money in the salesperson.
6. **Yes.**
7. **Yes.** You have a right to maintain the standards that your other salespeople are observing. Salespeople who do not carry their weight drag the team down.
8. **Yes.** This is sometimes true. One purpose of counseling is to remove any uncertainty about what is to be done and how.
9. **Yes.** You know that you have the weight of evidence on your side.

10. **Yes.**
11. **No.** It's normal for salespeople to have some negative feelings about being given unfavorable feedback, even though they may realize it is necessary. There may be embarrassment, anger, or humiliation. Expect a negative reaction and let it be expressed. Once it is out in the open, the two of you can work on solutions.
12. **No.** Forget what you can't see or measure. Stick to behavior.
13. **Yes.** If you don't listen, you might miss learning something. Furthermore, the salesperson probably won't be ready to listen to you if you show indifference to what he or she has to say.
14. **Yes.**
15. **Yes.**
16. **Not sure.** You may not want to get deeply involved in the details of a personal problem. And you probably aren't qualified to deal with it anyway.
17. **Yes.**
18. **Not sure.** You should also check to make sure the employee completely understands the agreement. And, in a sense, a counseling session might not be a total success unless there is a desired change of behavior.
19. **No.** No one else should be present unless it is absolutely necessary. Only an extreme condition would warrant a third person—for example, if your relationship with the salesperson has been such that you have little credibility or authority with that particular salesperson.
20. **Yes.** If you try to deal with more than one problem in the same session, you may confuse exactly what is to be done and when.

The Benefits of Counseling

If there is even a remote possibility that you can salvage a failing salesperson, you should try. You owe it to the salesperson, to yourself, and to the company. Consider the following:

- *The cost of replacement.* You'll pay for recruiting, training, and possibly relocating a new employee. There'll be a

certain amount of expensive downtime while the new salesperson is getting oriented.

- *The salesperson is a partial asset.* The salesperson already
  knows the company; the product, service, or program; and
  the territory. If you could just find the key to improving
  his or her performance to an acceptable level, you'd undoubtedly enjoy productivity sooner than you'd get with a
  replacement.
- *Reassurance for your other salespeople.* They'd like to know
  that if they suffer a slump, you'd be willing to give them
  reasonable help and show reasonable patience.
- *Your reputation.* Employee failure and turnover aren't pluses
  for you. When you salvage a tough case, you're bound to
  be a hero.
- *Your obligation to the salesperson.* As a manager, you owe your
  salesperson a certain amount of help and guidance.

The Limits of Counseling

You've criticized; you've noted failings in appraisals. Still the
salesperson can't sustain the average weekly activity that you've
plainly and clearly established as the minimum acceptable, can't
seem to get the required number of new business appointments,
makes far too many fruitless callbacks, closes infrequently and
ineffectively, falls down on even routine service, accepts stalls and
objections. There are many types of failure. You've worked with
the person, coached, trained, explained. But the improvements
are slight, temporary, or nonexistent. There must be a limit to
how many times you extend a helping hand.

The following are red flags to warn you that much more
tolerance on your part can lead to big problems:

- You've criticized the salesperson repeatedly for a failing—
  at least two or three times—without seeing more than
  temporary correction.
- You have patiently and in detail shown the salesperson how
  to correct the problem and improve performance to an
  acceptable level.
- You've gotten feedback from the salesperson that convinces

you that the salesperson knows there is a problem and knows how to improve.

• You've provided a sufficient amount of time for the correction to be made, without seeing success.

Counseling is the final opportunity for both of you to communicate clearly what is happening and what must happen. If it does not happen then, each of you knows what is in store— transfer, demotion, or termination (more about how to fire later in this chapter).

Preparing for Counseling

First assemble your documentation, whatever establishes that there is a deficiency: activity reports, correspondence, productivity records, and so on. It helps to have some evidence of your previous negative feedback: dates of your criticism, memos to the file summarizing the conversation and what was agreed to, perhaps an appraisal form if it is relevant. Documentation has at least a threefold benefit: (1) it helps you avoid arguments, (2) it justifies your decision to terminate the salesperson should he or she try to take you to court for discrimination or wrongful discharge, and (3) it cuts down on the stress you feel. There is always some stress in a counseling situation, for you as well as the salesperson. Counseling is seldom accomplished without some pain.

Schedule enough time to do the job right. Counseling is not something you can polish off in a short time, so be prepared to take as much time as necessary for both of you to say everything you want to say and to hear what you need to hear. You'll need privacy—your office or the salesperson's, a hotel room, even a car if that's all that's available.

Don't give much notice. A prolonged lead time means that stress and anxiety will build in both of you. It's best simply to announce, "I'd like you to be in my office tomorrow morning first thing. We need to talk." Or, "I'm going to be in your city tomorrow evening. I'd appreciate it if you would plan to spend some time with me." If possible, avoid giving notice of a Monday meeting on the Friday before. The consequence is a weekend of misery.

The Counseling Sequence

When you sit down with a salesperson, get right to the point. Don't lead off with small talk or pleasantries. You are engaged in very serious business. Here's a six-step sequence that you'll find helpful:

1. *State the problem.* "We agreed that you would maintain an average of twelve new business calls each week." Or, "I made clear to you that your territory would have to produce at least $20,000 of volume each week." Or, "Your minimum quota of new accounts for the first quarter was fifteen. That's what we discussed. You didn't make the quota, or the one we set for the quarter before, and it looks as if you won't make the thirteen we agreed on for this quarter."

In stating the problem, stick with the facts and the salesperson's behavior. As I have cautioned before, stay away from attitudes or motives. This is an example of an inappropriate description of a deficiency: "If you think I'm going to let you get away with so-so production, you've got another thing coming." The suggestion that the salesperson is trying to put something over on you is insulting. Here's another comment that is unsuitable: "What it comes down to, I guess, is that you just don't have the will to succeed." You really have no way of knowing whether the person lacks an essential quality. You'll get less argument from the salesperson if you describe the situation strictly in terms of what you can see.

2. *Get the salesperson's agreement on the problem.* Don't plunge ahead without checking that the salesperson sees the problem as you do. There may have been a misunderstanding. "Wait a minute," she says, "when you proposed twelve calls for new business, I said that I couldn't manage that at first, that I would have to work up to that. I thought you said that would be OK. You said eight the first week, then nine, and so on." When there seems to be a disagreement, you can respond, "All right, maybe I've misunderstood. Tell me how you see the situation." On the other hand, if you have documentation, you can support your view: "Well, here's the letter I wrote you immediately following our goal-setting talk. It plainly says twelve from week one."

It's also possible that the salesperson could say at this stage, "Look, I just don't see this as being as important as you do." Somewhere along the line you didn't convey how important the quotas or the goals are to you. The counseling session is the time to close that gap.

3. *Listen.* Accept the possibility that the salesperson has a story to tell or must vent some emotion. A negative reaction to counseling is quite normal, so don't try to rush through it. For example, your salesperson might say, "I know you want that volume, but I told you before I need extra help. Sam Carstair can do it easily because he has more experience than I do. I sometimes feel as if you are ignoring me." You don't have to agree with what the salesperson says, but accept that he or she believes or feels that way. This interview will help you determine what the salesperson needs and whether that perception is justified. After all, the salesperson may be trying to enlist your sympathy out of desperation.

4. *Consider extenuating circumstances.* For example, the territory is changing. Business is moving out of the inner city for the suburbs, and out of the salesperson's area. There may indeed be insufficient knowledge or skill that you failed to detect before. There could be personal problems. You find out for the first time that his spouse is bedridden, and that he must stay home in the morning to get the children ready for school. Or there might have been service snafus in the home office that caused her extra grief.

5. *Design an action plan for improvement.* "We both agree that there is a problem. Let's look for an alternative that would make us both happy." You may very well want to stick to the twelve new business calls per week, but you set a progressive goal: "Right now you're averaging only seven. Within one month I want that up to twelve. Each of those four weeks, you'll make one or two more such calls than you did the week before. At the end of the four weeks, you'll be up to twelve. And I expect you to stay at that level."

The action plan may include the means. To illustrate:

One reason you didn't bring in the volume is a lack of good appointments and, as you point out, you have problems getting appointments because you are weak on the telephone. I'll schedule two days with you the week after next, and we'll work on your telephone technique. When I arrive, you'll have an active prospect list of 500 names. We'll work from that. Starting the following week, I want you to make 100 phone calls each week. At the end of six weeks, your volume should be up to the $20,000. It'll have to be.

6. *Get the salesperson's agreement on the action plan.* One way to pin down the agreement is to have a written record of the plan (see the Performance Improvement Plan reproduced here for a sample). There are basically three things the salesperson must understand and agree to: (1) what is to be done, (2) in what time period it is to be done, and (3) what happens if it is not done in that time period. Have the salesperson sign and keep a copy of the plan.

Be careful about describing the sanction you intend to impose if the salesperson's efforts are not successful, because what you promise is what you'll have to deliver. If you threaten termination, then you must follow through, unless there are cogent reasons to change the sanction. Your credibility is at stake.

Following is a checklist you'll want to keep handy to help you do a good job in your next counseling session.

Counseling Skills Checklist

☐ In my counseling sessions, I try to control the discussion.
☐ I recognize that the salesperson being counseled has needs and wants that I should respect and resources I should call upon in arriving at a solution.
☐ I make sure I know in advance what I want from a counseling session.
☐ I consider myself a persuader trying to get the action I want from the counseled employee, although I will not hesitate to insist that my standards be followed if the salesperson seems disinclined to accept them.
☐ During a session, I am alert to the possibility that the salesperson will try to get me off a course of action.

(text continues on page 122)

Performance Improvement Plan

Salesperson: _____

Feedback history (dates on which the salesperson received criticism regarding the problem): _____

_____

Description of the improvement plan: _____

_____

_____

_____

_____

_____

_____

Target dates for the completion of each step and overall goal:

_____

_____

_____

_____

_____

_____

Follow-up date for the next review: _____

Signed: _____
                     (Salesperson)

_____
                     (Manager)

☐ I work to involve employees in finding a solution to a problem or in finding alternative behavior.

☐ I show that I respect the employee even though I disapprove of his or her actions or behavior.

☐ I accept the employee's opinions or beliefs in an explanation without necessarily agreeing with it.

☐ I anticipate that the counseled salesperson will have some negative feelings.

☐ I accept the employee's belief that he or she has a right to those negative emotions, even though I don't agree.

☐ In counseling, I talk about a salesperson's behavior, not attitudes or motives.

☐ In counseling, I believe that listening can be just as important as talking.

☐ I especially listen to learn something about the operation.

☐ When I listen, I maintain eye contact, look attentive without smiling or frowning, and don't interrupt.

☐ When a salesperson has difficulty talking, I ask encouraging questions to get him or her to open up.

☐ I limit distractions while the salesperson talks.

☐ When I give feedback, I am specific in telling the salesperson what I expect.

☐ When I feel anger during the session, I let it show; I do not pretend that I am not angry.

☐ When a salesperson shows anger or resistance, I let him or her express it fully before we start to work on an action plan.

☐ I try never to start a counseling session without appropriate documentation.

☐ I realize it is important to ask questions to determine how much the salesperson hears and understands what I say.

☐ I assume that it is my responsibility to spell out exactly what I want of the salesperson as a result of the counseling.

☐ I believe that when I convey my expectation that things will go a certain way, I increase the probability that they will in fact go that way.

Another Chance?

If, as the end of the improvement period approaches, the salesperson hasn't been successful in raising the performance level to meet your standards, you have to make a serious decision: Do you extend the period of probation, or do you announce that it's all over? Here's a checklist to help you decide whether to give your floundering salesperson another chance. Under the following conditions, you might consider extending the period:

- ☐ The salesperson has experienced personal or family problems, such as illness, that have interfered with his or her attempts to perform better.
- ☐ The economic environment has turned down and the whole team has had problems maintaining production.
- ☐ There have been problems in the company with quality, failure in service, or home office backup that have affected everyone in the field.
- ☐ For whatever reasons, you have been unable to provide your probationary employee with the monitoring and help that you had expected to give.
- ☐ There has been a product modification or price increase that has muddied the water and affected performance in general.
- ☐ A natural disaster such as an earthquake or flood has disrupted business.

Unless you can point to some general inhibitor such as those above, there's no way to rationalize your decision to extend. If you believe that you have been fair and helpful and reasonably patient without getting the results you expected, it's time to bite the bullet.

When Counseling Fails

When all your efforts fail to bring about an improvement in performance, it's time to remove that person from your sales team.

Firing a Salesperson

If you've promised that continuing failure will lead to termination, then you must fire the salesperson when it becomes quite clear that he or she is unwilling or unable to take the steps that are necessary to improve. There is no substitute for a face-to-face session. Some managers use the telephone or the mail to convey the bad news, but delivering the decision in person is more humane.

Get right to the point: "For some time, I've been disappointed that you have not met my standards for weekly activity and volume. You and I have talked a number of times about it. But there hasn't been any improvement. I have to let you go." The salesperson may want to talk about your decision, may even hope to talk you out of it. Be prepared to listen, but before you give the other person the floor, say, "I'll listen to whatever you have to say, but I want you to understand that I will not change my decision. That is irreversible." You may have to remind the other person from time to time that your decision is final.

Is there a time that is more suitable than others to wield the axe? Probably the best time to fire someone is early in the week, because the person can start making contacts immediately. Firing on a Friday afternoon may mean a whole weekend of self-pity or at least helplessness because there's no way to make business contacts and line up interviews.

Some managers like to tell the salesperson what they will say if prospective employers call them for references or information about the salesperson's record. One manager routinely answers inquiries from other companies with, "It wasn't the right fit, and we agreed to disagree." That statement conveys the message, "He wasn't successful here." It suggests nothing about whether the person could achieve more elsewhere.

If you must announce someone's departure to your own people, avoid the usual nonsense such as, "She left to pursue other interests." This isn't the time for camouflage and euphemisms. Just say, "She's no longer with us," and leave it at that. They all know. And you'll acquire credibility in their eyes. You want a winning team, and you're willing to take painful measures to get it.

Transferring an Unsuccessful Salesperson

Firing may be the most feasible option, but consider the possibility of transferring a salesperson to a job more suited to his or her particular temperament and talents. One such successful transfer happened while I was with an insurance company as a field group benefits manager. One of our Midwest specialists—bright, articulate, likable—had been unsuccessful in bringing in the expected level of volume. The sales manager worked with him in a very concerned manner, but it eventually became evident that the young man was in the wrong job. Unquestionably he had fine talents, and the sales manager felt that it would be a loss to the company to simply let him go. They found a job for him in the group department in the home office, and he functioned beautifully. He knew the business, he knew the company, he knew many of the people in the field. Those inside and in the field found him a pleasure to work with. It was a fine example of salvaging an asset.

If you're going to lose someone as a salesperson, consider the possibility that the person who doesn't sell well may shine elsewhere in the company:

- *The home office.* In the above example, it worked out wonderfully.
- *Sales training.* Your ex-seller knows the challenges and problems of the field better than any inside trainer who has never been outside. Such a person will have a rapport and a credibility with your salespeople that are enviable.
- *Marketing.* Your ex-salesperson may need a bit of broadening and educating to function in your home office marketing operation, but again, such a person has highly relevant experience.
- *Nonsales and nonmarketing.* Your ex-seller may have technical knowledge, such as chemistry or engineering, that could well be utilized elsewhere. Perhaps your failure may be a success in public relations or advertising.

The above are just thought-starters. Think about the advantages if you take the time to concern yourself with an unsuccessful salesperson. If you are gracious and generous in helping someone transfer, somebody will appreciate that you had the company's best interests in mind. And you'll have a good friend and ally inside. Who knows when your ex-salesperson can intervene for you or represent your interests?

Dealing With a Salesperson's Personal Problems

Now and then you may find that a salesperson's performance is slipping because of family problems or marital discord. Even worse, your salesperson may be addicted to drugs or alcohol. Most managers are not qualified to deal with these kinds of problems. About all you can do is listen. First, however, make sure that the salesperson really wants you to hear such problems and make sure also that you are willing to become involved.

If you are uncomfortable when a salesperson begins to divulge intimate information, stop the conversation. You can say, "Look, Phyllis, I know you need to talk, but you also need someone to listen. I'm just not qualified to help you. You need to talk to someone who is." Then gently suggest that the person in pain seek professional guidance.

Even if you are not uncomfortable hearing personal matters, you should probably stop the conversation long enough to say, "Are you sure you want me to hear these things? I don't want you to be uncomfortable later." From that point on, it's a judgment call. You may decide to let the salesperson go on. On the other hand, you may prefer to urge that the salesperson talk to someone more qualified. It really depends on your relationship with the salesperson. If it is warm and trusting, then you will probably feel easy about being an audience.

The situation becomes more complicated when you have to do something about the person's productivity while he or she is so burdened. Again, much depends on the person's track record. If it has been very good up until now, you may feel that you can afford to ease up on the performance standards and requirements temporarily. However, don't hesitate to convey the message that you will be understanding up to a point:

> Carl, I can see you're awfully upset, and you need some time to get things sorted out. I know how conscientious you are about your work. I'm sure that you'll want to get some help to find a solution soon, so that you can carry on as before. For the time being, I'd like you to stay close to me, check in every few days to let me know how you are progressing. I'm convinced that the faster you can get back to devoting your full energies to your work, the better off you'll be.

With such a statement, you serve the interests of both of you, and you have some room to maneuver. So does Carl. If the problems go on and Carl's performance continues to suffer, you'll have to decide how much more tolerant you can be. However, if Carl is not a steady and admirable producer, you may have to be more assertive to protect your interests, more insistent that the salesperson get help. As you can see, there are no hard-and-fast rules. Your judgment will be related to the salesperson, his or her history, and the seriousness of the problem. And you might feel comfortable relying on Carl's judgment: "If you feel that you need a leave of absence, I'll find ways to cover your accounts until you are ready to resume selling."

Alcohol and Substance Abuse

There are, however, some rather firm rules about tolerating drug addiction or alcoholism. (These days, cross addiction is rather common among abusers.) The first rule is that under no circumstances should you try to counsel the salesperson yourself. That takes professional skill, and even then can be a sticky issue. The rule applies even if the salesperson is a friend and has had a long relationship with you.

Don't attempt to label the person an addict or an alcoholic. Don't even discuss the nature of the problem except as it relates to the salesperson's performance: "Your activity is down"; "You're missing too much time from work"; "The figures from your territory are dismal." You undoubtedly know why the salesperson has gone into a slump; it's hard to keep drinking and drugging quiet forever. But deal only with the behavior on the job. If it is not what you want, you have a right to demand that it change.

Counsel on performance only. Require that the person get outside help if you think the problem is personal. There are treatment programs and employee assistance specialists, so let them take over. Your message is: "Whatever it takes to get back on track, you'd better avail yourself of it. If you don't shape up and produce up to quota, I'm going to have to terminate you."

Follow through on your warning. People who are abusers of drugs and alcohol are very skilled at promising to get help. They will tell you whatever they think you want to hear. But in your conversations with them, stick to productivity. If it improves, fine. If it doesn't, terminate. One final note: You may have to tolerate an absence of several weeks, should the person enter a rehabilitation program.

KEY TO CHAPTER 5

The last step in managing the motivation of your salespeople is to reward them. When people do things right, and do the right things, don't miss opportunities to say, in words or in actions, "I really appreciate the effort you've made. Thank you."

How effectively do you use the rewards you have available to you? The following self-assessment will tell you.

Understanding Rewards and Using Them Effectively

Before reading this last chapter on rewards, you'll find it interesting and useful to assess your knowledge and application of rewards for good performance by agreeing or disagreeing with the following statements.

	Agree	Disagree
1. Most managers probably fail to take full advantage of the power they possess in rewarding good performance.	_____	_____
2. Rewarding good performance means the same as the psychological term *positive reinforcement*.	_____	_____
3. When salespeople value the rewards you give for good performance, they are likely to repeat that performance.	_____	_____
4. When we criticize a person's performance, we are negatively reinforcing it.	_____	_____
5. Negative reinforcement is a major reason why managers see disappointing performance by subordinates.	_____	_____
6. If you want to understand why a person behaves a certain way, look for the reward the person believes will result from acting in that manner.	_____	_____
7. When people don't feel rewarded for what they do, they'll often change their behavior, for good or worse.	_____	_____

Agree   Disagree

8. The annual bonus or merit increase can be very effective in increasing motivation if it is used wisely. _____ _____

9. Positive work attitudes should be rewarded as well as actual performance. _____ _____

10. The more specific you are in describing the behavior you are rewarding, the more helpful it is to the salesperson, who now knows what to continue to do. _____ _____

11. A reward given once for successful new behavior by a salesperson may not be sufficient to make that behavior ongoing. _____ _____

12. Praise as a reward is usually not very effective because salespeople see it as cheap and readily available. _____ _____

13. The rule is always to praise in public and criticize in private. _____ _____

14. When salespeople change their ways and become more successful through new behavior, that behavior should be reinforced periodically to ensure its permanence. _____ _____

15. There is no such thing as too much praise. _____ _____

16. An effective way to reward good sales performance is to give a salesperson more responsibilities. _____ _____

17. Providing training to good performers can be seen as a reward. _____ _____

18. A popular type of reward for good performance is greater freedom from supervision and to choose one's own way of working. _____ _____

19. When you take the time to sit down occasionally with good performers to encourage them to talk about their plans for the future, you are bestowing a valuable reward on them. _____ _____

20. Professional growth is a powerful motivator, and the opportunity for it is a powerful reward. _____ _____

Analysis

1. **Agree.** In thirty years of working with managers, I have seldom seen managers who truly appreciate the power they have to

encourage good performance in their subordinates by rewarding that performance.

2. **Agree.**
3. **Agree.** People do what they feel rewarded for doing. Of course, you must bear in mind that the reward you give must be seen as valuable by them.
4. **Disagree.** When you reinforce negatively, you do nothing. It's the absence of reinforcement. Sometimes criticism can be construed as punishment or, to use the psychological term, *aversive conditioning.*
5. **Agree.** When managers fail to positively reinforce their salespeople's desirable behavior, they shouldn't be surprised when that behavior stops because the salespeople don't feel rewarded for performing that way.
6. **Agree.** The reward may not always be obvious to you, but it's there. And if you want to change someone's behavior, you must change the reward.
7. **Agree.** See number 5 above.
8. **Disagree.** To be effective, rewards must immediately follow the good performance and must be seen as a result of that performance. Once a year is not enough for most people. In fact, many annual corporate compensation increases are, in the minds of employees, too little and too late to have much motivational value.
9. **Disagree.** Stick with behavior and performance; forget attitudes. You can't see them or measure them.
10. **Agree.**
11. **Agree.** For a new behavior to take shape, frequent reinforcing is often necessary. After the behavior has taken root, it should be reinforced intermittently to make it permanent.
12. **Disagree.** Honest praise from a credible boss stands on its own as a potent reinforcer. People love praise.
13. **Disagree.** The word *always* is the problem. Sometimes public praise of a good performer can cause a sour taste in the mouths of other salespeople if they believe they are not playing on a level field. If they believe the praised performer enjoys advantages, they'll discount your praise. And there are occasions when behavior warrants public criticism. In certain group situations, a member's behavior might be obstructive or even demeaning to others in a meeting. Such behavior has to be stopped if the meeting is to proceed constructively, so the offender must be told how disruptive his or her actions or words are.
14. **Agree.** See number 11 above.

15. **Disagree.** There is no such thing as too much *deserved* and *proportionate* praise, but if other people don't believe that the person deserves such effusive plaudits, they may suspect that the manager is playing favorites.
16. **Agree.** Most people who perform well respond well to increased responsibility, challenge, and the opportunity to grow. They also like the variety that comes with differing or greater responsibility. No one likes to do the same thing year after year.
17. **Agree.** Training adds new skills and knowledge, and that growth is an effective motivator.
18. **Agree.** More control over one's work and methods is a reward many people value greatly.
19. **Agree.** People respond favorably to the interest you take in them and their careers when you counsel them for long-term growth and progress.
20. **Agree.** Growth and progress are strong motivating forces in most people.

5

Giving Rewards to Make the Change Permanent

The most potent tool you have in gaining the kind of sales productivity you want is rewards. Your reward power is limited only by what you make of it. This is one of the best-kept management secrets in business today. In my thirty years of experience dealing with managers and being one myself, I've seen little recognition that rewards provide the key to getting the results managers want.

The great Harvard psychologist B. F. Skinner taught pigeons in his laboratory to obtain food for themselves by pecking on a lever. Once the pigeon discovered that a peck would bring a food pellet, the bird would try it again. When it happened for the second and third time, the pigeon realized that it was on to a very good thing. One peck, one pellet. The pigeon's behavior was being positively reinforced. It was getting a reward. Skinner called the relationship between the behavior and the reward *operant conditioning*. We're more used to the term *positive reinforcement*: When behavior is reinforced with a reward that the doer finds valuable, that behavior tends to be repeated.

It works with pigeons, and it works with people. Of course, the difference between pigeons and people is that the pigeon has to discover the desired behavior on its own. But we managers can sit down with our subordinates and say, "This is what I want from you." And when we get it, we reinforce it. We reward it. We say to the salesperson, "That's great." When we get a repetition, we reinforce it. The subordinate presumably continues to employ the new behavior, and it becomes permanent.

That's the way it's supposed to work. Unfortunately, it often doesn't. There's nothing wrong with the psychological principle. Rather, the fault lies with us. We get busy and we forget to reinforce the new behavior. Or we reinforce it in ineffective ways, so that the salesperson doesn't feel rewarded. When the behavior isn't reinforced positively, that is, isn't recognized or rewarded at all, psychologists say that we are reinforcing negatively—nothing is coming from us. And generally that's what happens in the subordinate—nothing. When the pigeon doesn't get food from pecking, the bird stops pecking. When subordinates don't feel rewarded, they may revert to previous behavior.

In reality, most managers do not grasp this essential fact: People do what they feel rewarded for doing. If one of your salespeople is making ten calls a week when you want twelve, you say, "I expect you to make the extra effort to call on two more prospects next week." So the salesperson does, and you say nothing. Next week he makes twelve calls again, and you say nothing. The next week, you shouldn't be surprised if he falls back to ten calls. You have negatively reinforced your salesperson.

How to Reward

If you want your reward to be most effective, you must follow certain rules regarding reinforcement:

• *Reward soon after the event.* You'll notice that this is the same advice as for criticizing. It's necessary that your salespeople see a direct connection between what they have done and the reward so they know what to keep on doing. When your subordinate reports making twelve calls, you should be on the phone without delay saying, "I appreciate that special effort you made in adding two more calls to your activity." The next week, the salesperson calls on twelve more prospects and immediately hears from you: "Great. You now know you can make twelve calls a week instead of ten." After two or three more weeks, you call again: "I just want you to know how pleased I am to see that you are maintaining your average of twelve calls a week."

• *Be specific.* In the preceding paragraph, you'll notice that I advocate describing the salesperson's good behavior. It's not enough to say, "Great job. Keep it up." What's great? What should he keep up? The more specific you are in describing the behavior, the more precisely your salesperson knows what to continue to do.

• *Stick to behavior.* You can't go wrong if you talk only about what a salesperson does. It's visible and measurable. You can get into a lot of trouble when you try to compliment an attitude. To illustrate, a manager has seen a gradual increase in a salesperson's accomplishments. There's no question that she has been trying. Of course, the manager is very pleased. He means well when he says to her, "Perri, it's so wonderful to see how your attitude has changed for the better." But she frowns and asks, "What do you mean?" Now a bit flustered, he responds, "You know, you really seem to want to be a success in selling." "I always wanted to be a success," she says, her voice getting edgy. "I wasn't sure how, so I had a few discussions with Walt Traynor. I figured that our number-one guy would have something useful to teach me, and he did." This manager has come across as insensitive and more than a bit condescending.

Just as in selling, the wrong word or phrase can do you in. Here's another manager who wants to recognize his salesman's improved performance. He says, "Steve, it's a pleasure to see that you've become so much more careful in your interviews." Steve is a bit bewildered and asks, "What do you mean that I'm more careful?" The manager tries to salvage the situation by saying, "What I mean is that you're more careful about picking up buying signals from prospects during your presentations." But it's too late. "I was always careful," Steve argues, "but I've learned how to listen better. Being careful had nothing to do with it." This manager would have been better off not saying anything, because he botched the feedback.

• *Be consistent.* When you want to shape new behavior, you have to follow its manifestation with some kind of reward—always. You have to be consistent with your reinforcement to get the best results.

Most reward systems in businesses seem to ignore the above realities. Salary or merit increases and bonuses are often given once a year. Thus, in January the company tells its employees that it really appreciates them, and here's some money to prove it. But presumably they've been doing a good job for the past twelve months. Why do they have to wait so long to get the goodie?

Salespeople, they say, don't have to go through all this. After all, salespeople usually get some kind of incentive when they close business, and that money should provide positive feedback. It does. But unless it reaches the salespeople soon after, instead of on next month's commission statement, it's behind the times. The same can be said for the monthly production report. It's too far after the fact. The rewards would be much more effective if they reached the successful salespeople soon after the event and properly reflected specific accomplishments. It's doubtful that we can change the behavior of the compensation specialists, whose interest lies in serving the needs of the system rather than the needs of those who make it work. But managers of field salespeople can do much to fill the gap.

The Potency of Praise

Perhaps you don't have money at your disposal, and maybe you can't speed up the reward system in your company. But you do have an inexhaustible supply of a wonderful nonmonetary reward that almost every salesperson wants and never gets enough of: praise.

Of course, as with anything, there are some conditions that must be present to make it work. First, you need to follow the recommendations that I cited earlier. Second, the praise should be proportionate to the accomplishment. If it's too little or too muted, the salesperson feels cheated; too much or too effusive, and the salesperson may feel manipulated. Finally, the salesperson has to respect and trust the manager in order for the praise to be meaningful.

You have to be on the alert not to give excessive praise when you have accomplished much with a salesperson and the salesperson's success reflects on you. One sales manager I knew was asked to try to salvage a failing salesman from another division. The manager tried and succeeded in helping the salesman attain a decent, not spectacular, level of productivity. But the manager's praise of the salesman was overblown. Actually, the manager's praise was a way of patting himself on the back for saving what everyone thought was a hopeless case. But the salesman believed it all and became insufferable. Others on the sales force resented the special attention he got and felt that so much praise was unjustified. All they had done, they complained, was to produce well all along.

Where to Praise

You often hear the counsel, "Praise in public, criticize in private." But as is true with any generalization, there are some exceptions. Generally, you won't have too much argument against praising people publicly for their performance, so long as the others on the team are playing on level ground. If they don't have the same opportunities or resources, they may resent the special attention. In such a situation, it's proper *not* to praise. For example, one of my group insurance colleagues who opened a regional office for the entire southeastern part of the United States enjoyed certain distinct advantages over any other company group office in the country. His region consistently led the country in volume, which was duly reported in our monthly productivity reports, but no special kudos were directed his way. That was proper, since the rest of us did not enjoy the same benefits.

How to Praise Well

Your goal is for the person who is praised to feel good about the complimentary words and to make your other salespeople want praise as well. And, of course, you don't want them to resent the person who is the beneficiary of your appreciation. Here are some rules that will help, especially when you praise publicly:

• *Be alert to opportunity.* When your salespeople do something that is praiseworthy, don't miss the chance to recognize it. Soon people will understand that you'll express your appreciation for good work. You don't have to tell good salespeople that they are special every day. But when someone does something special, don't let the accomplishment go unrewarded.

> Mark Spencer capped a six-month campaign to close the Fran-Mart chain of 308 stores. He managed to beat out seven major competitors. It was hard fought, but worth it. We'll all see a boost in the division volume this year, and I've already received a grateful letter from our president. Now when you pass a Fran-Mart outlet, you can take pride in knowing that we are a major supplier.

*   *   *

> I think that most of you know that we've been using Shirley Twomey's territory to train our new salespeople. Shirley has had responsibility for seeing that they get actual experience in the trenches. During the past year, Shirley has helped train four new additions to our staff, and all four are now in their territories making names for themselves. Congratulations to them and especially to Shirley, who not only turns in an exceptional volume but turns out fine salespeople.

If you are tempted to think that your salespeople may not regard such praise highly, my experience suggests otherwise. I still remember specific praise that I received ten, twenty, even thirty or more years ago. People like praise. It sticks.

• *Be persistent.* Periodically tell your people who have made improvements how much you appreciate them keeping the effort up.

> I get a great deal of satisfaction, Jill, out of your activity reports. You'll remember the day when I told you I thought you could achieve a closing ratio of one out of every three calls. You looked astonished. But now you're doing it on a regular basis. In fact, judging by the past three weeks, you're edging up to one out of every 2.8 calls. Congratulations! What kind of a closing ratio goal would you like to set now?

*   *   *

> I enjoyed sitting down with you at your computer, Trent, and

seeing how complete and up-to-date your prospect files are. I hope you don't mind my recalling last spring when you and I had a serious discussion about the shape of your files. You told me then you didn't see yourself as a "file clerk." But you gritted your teeth and did what I asked you to do. I thought you did a great job then, and I'm immensely pleased that you have kept those files impeccably. I know you're pleased, because, as you told me, you think that your jump in business over the last quarter has a lot to do with your file keeping. I think so too.

Both of the above managers could have used a memo to convey more permanent praise. The written word is a useful supplement to spoken praise. It's more lasting. The recipient can look at it several times and relish it or show it to others. On one occasion, my boss showed up at my door with a memo in which she repeated some nice words that she had spoken an hour before. I was touched that she had gone to the extra effort to make her words permanent.

• *Be clear.* Keep your message clear and focused. If it's performance you want, praise it; reward it. But praise only when the performance truly merits it. Managers sometimes issue confusing messages. Consider the case of a manager publicly praising good old Joe who hasn't missed a day's work in ten years. Unfortunately, Joe's coworkers know that Joe does mediocre work at best. What they hear is that all they have to do to gain favor with the boss is to show up regularly. In sum, decide what is important to you, what you are going to praise, and stick with that element. Don't muddy your messages.

• *Be proportionate.* Sometimes you may be tempted to give excessive praise to someone to express your compassion or friendly feelings. If you do, you risk losing credibility not only with your other salespeople but also with the recognized subordinate, who knows that such extravagant words aren't deserved.

• *Be specific.* When you describe what you admire, everyone gets the message about what you value. When you say, "Charlie, your persistence is marvelous," that doesn't have the impact of, "Charlie, you're tough and I like that. You really hang in there. Three times the prospect said he had to leave for a meeting, and you didn't budge." Writers are frequently told that they "write well." But what does that mean? When someone says, "You write so clearly and concisely and make your points quickly and convincingly, which shows good thinking," then you understand. When you are specific about what you like, your feedback to your salespeople doesn't all sound the same.

Other Types of Rewards

If you have money to give, more base salary or a bonus, fine. Cash is a reward that's always appreciated, especially when it closely follows good performance. But there are many other ways to show your appreciation for productivity that you can extend year-round. The three major rewards you should consider are:

1. More work
2. More of you
3. More training

Let's look at each in detail.

More Work

More work obviously means more challenging work and greater responsibilities. Most salespeople are grateful for a challenge, since they grow tired doing the same kinds of work over and over. If they're ambitious, a job that becomes easier with more competence will not be a turn-on. Here are some possibilities you can consider:

• *Job enlargement.* The technical or psychological term for this is *horizontal loading.* Essentially you combine the functions that a salesperson presently performs with other functions on the sales level. For example, a salesperson sells only some of the products or programs or calls on only certain accounts and not others. You expand the salesperson's responsibilities to include these other products or accounts. Another example of enlargement would be a larger area to cover: from five zip code zones to eight. Enlargement usually entails more quantity rather than a different quality.

> I'm splitting up Cal's old territory, now that he has retired. You get the west half, and John gets the east part. Both of you have done such a terrific job this year, I think you deserve a chance to make more money.

*   *   *

> You've been selling the associate memberships so well. We think you ought to have a chance at the executive memberships as well. That way, when you walk into a company now, you can offer them everything.

Job enlargement is a legitimate motivational tool, and for salespeople, it can be a fine reward for good performance. But be sure that you tie the expansion of responsibility to increased status and a recognition of achievement.

• *Job enrichment.* Just as job enlargement is horizontal loading, job enrichment is *vertical loading*. Your message to the salesperson is, "Because you have done such a good job with your present responsibilities, I'll give you some responsibility that actually belongs at a higher level." It's not necessarily a promotion. You're just giving the salesperson some functions that normally aren't performed at his or her level. What are some examples? Training; planning or even conducting a meeting for your salespeople; working on a special project with someone in the home office; chairing a task force to design a product modification; consulting with the marketing research people; preparing a report recommending solutions for sales problems. Be alert to work functions that you would normally perform that can be delegated to a superior performer. In fact, when you no longer regard some duties as challenging for you, you ought to start looking for subordinates who will.

More of You

A second type of generic reward is more of you. You may not think about it much, but you are one of the most effective rewards you can give for good performance, especially if your salespeople respect you. If they hold you in esteem, your esteem for high producers is a reward that they will cherish. There are a number of ways in which you can establish a special relationship with your leading salespeople:

• *Informal relationship.* You have at least a business friendship and discuss family matters, sports, books, and current events as well as business. You make yourself accessible and find time for an exceptional salesperson. You convey the message that you value the salesperson on more than one level.

• *Consulting.* You seek the person's advice or expertise on a proposed project, a new salesperson, or some aspect of the company that involves you. Of course, you must sincerely solicit the opinion with every intention of incorporating the person's thinking into your own, if possible.

• *Career counseling.* You show special concern for the salesperson's future and career progress. You occupy a vantage point; you know what is happening in the company, the opportunities that may be opening up, prerequisites for greater responsibility, and the promising career paths. Your caring counsel can help to ensure continued motivated performance. (See "Coaching for Growth" later in this chapter.)

• *Inside information.* There is never quite enough information circulating in the company to satisfy employees who are truly involved. You usually have more of it than your salespeople. Without passing along confidential or hurtful information or gossip, you can provide inside information about imminent announcements about a new product or service, promotions that are in the works, or an impending acquisition that has not yet been announced. Your taking the time to communicate advance or not readily available information confers extra status on the salesperson.

• *Your concern.* You might say, "You've been working awfully long hours lately." Or, "You really knocked yourself out on that Wells project. I'd like you to find a way to take it easy for a bit. I don't want you to burn out or become exhausted." Perhaps you recommend that the salesperson take a long weekend or start thinking about a vacation. Be alert to clues in the salesperson's behavior that might point to fatigue, worry, boredom, or excessive exuberance. Comment on what you see: "In the last talk we had, you seemed very preoccupied. Am I right? Is there anything I can do?" That way you can show your concern without seeming to meddle. There may not really be anything wrong, but your concern won't go to waste.

• *Personal information.* You may talk with a key salesperson with whom you have a good working relationship about a problem you have at work, or a child who is causing you some concern, or your vacation plans. You don't want to divulge information that would embarrass either of you, but communicating on a personal level conveys the message, "I value you as a working friend." Your esteem for the productive salesperson becomes quite clear.

Some managers unfortunately dilute the impact of this very important and powerful personal reward by confusing the issue of what it takes to be close to the boss. It's natural to feel more warmth and friendliness toward certain personalities than toward others, regardless of sales performance. With some people the chemistry is there; you have much to share. But consider the price you pay when, regardless of the salesperson's professional value and productivity, you extend yourself toward particular salespeople. Others who do not feel close to you will come to believe that the basis for getting on the boss's good side is something quite removed from excellent selling. Therefore, if you want to be a reward yourself, keep your regard for salespeople who perform well on a distinct level from your personal good feelings toward some of them. Confine your favors, perks, close attention, and public esteem to those who do a good job for you. It may be difficult at times to deemphasize a friendship in favor of showing that you value performance and professionalism even more in your role as manager.

More Training

Training can be seen as a reward. Of course, most of this book is about the training that you provide to your salespeople on a continuing basis. This section concerns itself more with formal training and education—the type that you very likely don't offer.

Training programs sometimes suggest a negative message. People who are sent to them frequently get the idea that they are there to get "fixed" in some way. So managers are often surprised when I insist that their subordinates can view training as a reward, if it is presented in the proper way. For example, one day I was called into my boss's office. She held out a brochure from the University of Virginia advertising a three-day workshop on public-speaking skills. She said, "I thought you might want to go to this. Someday the skills could come in handy." I saw the invitation as a reward, because there was little chance I would do much public speaking in my present job. I was—and am—grateful for the workshop. I do much public speaking now. She was correct.

Most people are eager to grow. They want to believe that they can be better at what they do next year than they are this year; or that they can do more, that they can learn new skills. Most training and education that you pay for will undoubtedly be work related. But with your outstanding people, don't rule out courses, seminars, workshops, and lectures that broaden the perspective and deepen the thinking of your salespeople, even if the content of those programs doesn't directly and immediately affect how they work. When you're looking for educational and training opportunities for your exceptional producers, investigate these sources:

• *Your corporate training department.* Your special salesperson may be a trainee or a trainer. Are there skills-building programs that the salesperson might benefit from, such as writing courses, merchandising and advertising, public relations, customer service, almost anything related to marketing? It is not necessary that your salesperson have an immediate opportunity to apply the new knowledge, although that would be nice. Rather, the benefit comes from the salesperson's feeling that he or she is capable of moving up or in a different direction and that you are showing esteem and confidence by recommending the training.

You can probably negotiate with your training department to design and deliver some of this advanced training and education. If it doesn't already have such programs, it will undoubtedly be interested in preparing them, if clients are willing to underwrite them. Other managers will probably be interested in sending their high producers when they discover that such programs are available.

Don't overlook the benefits of lending your high producer part time or temporarily full time to the training department to act as adviser in developing programs or to actually deliver training modules or portions of them. For the field salesperson, the whole experience can be one of enormous growth, if only in that he or she is acquiring talent in developing and delivering training to others. It's very difficult to be a good trainer without appreciating it as a learning opportunity.

• *Outside seminars and workshops.* The American Management Association provides workshops for two, three, even five days in specialized areas of sales and marketing, as do a number of other organizations. Some universities also have external arms that offer short-term programs. The benefit isn't only the content that the presenter offers, but the contact and exchange with other people who are attending as well.

• *Courses at local colleges and universities.* Many educational institutions have discovered that continuing adult learning is a profitable field. They offer night and weekend programs in marketing and allied fields. Or a salesperson might benefit from computer courses or from a course dealing more with internal corporate functions than with field sales. Again, it's a judgment call on your part whether a program that doesn't pay off for you and your salesperson in immediate relevance and application can result in long-term gain, such as increased motivation and loyalty to you and the company. The intangible benefits may be worth much more than the short-term profits.

• *Detached service.* If, in the process of career counseling, you uncover a salesperson's desire to eventually move into other areas of corporate work, such as computer programming or finance, consider giving your exceptional producer a short-term assignment to one of these functional areas. Granted, you take the person out of the field for a week and risk providing an even greater temptation to eventually leave you, but you're doing something substantial to show your interest in the salesperson and gratitude for his or her productivity while in service to you. Actually, such a person may return to the field much wiser and more valuable in that the person's world view has been considerably broadened.

• *A special task force.* No doubt there are persistent, pervasive, stubborn problems that could be solved if anyone had the time to tackle them. Or perhaps they cross lines of authority, so that no one manager can get a mandate to do something about them. Then again, there are opportunities to change the way things are done now, to create innovations, if only people had the time. One thing that is evident about most busy, successful people is that they know how to make time, if they see a payoff. One way to get problems solved, decisions made, and changes launched is to create a task force that has such an issue as its focus. Offer your high producers a chance to sit on the task force, to deal with a challenge that no one else has dealt with successfully, and see what happens. True, some of your stars want only to achieve wealth and glory through selling, and that's fine. But others want a mix of rewards, and some of those people will see possibilities for themselves in a task force that has high visibility.

First you must make sure that they all know that a task force is not a committee. A committee deliberates and advises. A task force solves and, when necessary, creates the structure to keep the solution in force. Perhaps your company needs to overhaul its sales recruiting or its basic sales training; or sales territories need realignment; or marketing approaches need updating; or management selection needs formulating; or home office R&D, engineering, or production needs inputs from the people who sell what they produce. You gather your good producers and tell them, "Here's the situation. Come up with a better option." Give them authority, reasonable time and freedom, and let them show you what they can do. It will be a marvelous learning experience for them, and the company will benefit by their answers. If the project needs structure and staff, let them tell you how to set it up. Maybe there's a continuing role for them. I once sat on a task force that designed the product, set up the department to produce it, and even had a hand in how it was to be marketed. The experience gave an enormous boost to my career.

Coaching for Long-Term Growth

One of the most appreciated rewards you can provide a good performer is coaching him or her for long-term growth. It makes sense that your salespeople look to you for guidance in their development. You know them. You work with them. You've seen what they can do, and undoubtedly you have some opinions about what they are capable of doing in the future. You know the organization and the field. You usually know far better than your salespeople what their career paths are and will be.

Ben has been selling in Martha's division for eight years. On one of her periodic visits to Ben's territory, Martha schedules time to talk a bit about Ben's future, since Ben has been one of Martha's most important producers. The manager also realizes that Ben is ambitious and will probably look for a corporate career path in the home office. After making joint calls for the day, Martha invites Ben to join her for a drink at her hotel.

Martha: I mentioned this morning that I thought we ought to sit down this evening and talk a bit about what you may be looking forward to in the next few years. I suspect you've been thinking about where you want to be in the next three to five years.

Ben: Sure. I like what I'm doing now, but I have to be up-front, Martha. I don't want to spend the rest of my life in the trenches.

Martha: I accept that, although I want you to know that I regard you as one of my stars. You manage to exceed your quota by at least a quarter every year. That's outstanding. Of course, I know it's making you a lot of money. Look Ben, I won't pretend. I'll be sorry to lose you. I'd do anything reasonable to see you stay on. Also, you probably know this already, but you aren't likely to make the money you're making now when you leave the field.

Ben: Maybe not right away, but someday . . .

Martha: Someday, right. What do you think are your strengths that you can apply in another position?

Ben: No room for excessive modesty here. I'm quite proud of the way I relate to people. It makes selling a lot of fun for me, because every new person I meet is a challenge to me. How fast can I get on the prospect's wavelength? The whole matter of building rapport as fast as possible is exciting. Reading people's body language and both the verbal and nonverbal signals is a skill I've been developing over the years, and I'm getting pretty good at it.

Martha: That gives me a thought. I agree that you're very sharp in reading people. I watched you today quickly get on the good side of a couple of tough businessmen. Well, the thought I have is to carve out some time at the September meeting to let you hold a clinic on just that skill: building rapport. Say two or three hours in which you'd do a little talking and some facilitating, to get some of the others opened up. Would you mind sharing your secrets?

Ben: No, I'd be flattered. You remember I did that one session a couple of years back at the national sales meeting on developing large accounts. I really enjoyed that.

Martha: As I remember, it got good reviews too. Especially the part about doing the missionary work with users and influentials. I suspect it opened a lot of eyes about what you have to do to crack the major accounts—and keep them. Is it OK if I give you some of my preliminary conclusions?

Ben: Great.

Martha: All right. Yes, you do have a lot of strength in your flexibility. You can move this way or that, or rapidly change course. That's a tremendous asset for a salesperson, but it's also valuable in managing. We haven't made an announcement about Cliff Meyers, but he's going to retire at the end of the year. His district will be open. I think with some help and preparation you could probably step right into his shoes. You'd be working with seven or eight salespeople. How do you feel about the prospect of being a field manager?

Ben: It's a prospect. I'm glad you think I might be able to succeed Cliff.

Martha: It would be a change. And you'd grow into it. But what would help you, I think, is your flexibility. A lot of good salespeople aren't terribly adaptable. They find certain ways of doing things, and they don't have a great deal of tolerance. But you need tolerance and flexibility when you're working with other salespeople. So I believe that the same qualities that make you a successful salesman would help you be a good manager. OK, since I believe that it's good to offer you a choice, Mr. Prospect, instead of asking you to buy, let's talk about another possible option. You know that last month we announced that we're acquiring Kenmost. They have a sales force that's smaller than ours but has to be assimilated. We're going to be doing a heck of a lot of training, inside and in the field. You've already demonstrated that you're willing to share your best practices, and you do it well. Rob Kleiner is handling much of the sales training by himself. He and I were talking the other day, and we've agreed he's going to need some help. In fact, he mentioned you, but he wasn't sure you wanted to give up the front lines. It's a way to get inside. The job has some visibility. And who knows?

Ben: I like both options, Martha. But I have to tell you, the assistant sales training job is one I hadn't considered. I like it very much.

Martha: Tell you what. Here's what we can do. Suppose I call Cliff and ask him whether it's all right for you to spend two or three days with him to let you see how the old pro operates and whether you'd like to try managing. In addition, I'll talk to Rob, and either he'll come to visit you or you'll go to the home office for a day or so and have a good talk. No pressure. You can tell me then what you'd like to do. And we'll set some sort of schedule. You might start the training part time at first and continue selling, if that's the way you choose.

Martha sees her obligation as a long-term one of building a highly effective sales force, even if it means she has to help develop some of the key people right out of the field. But Martha knows the realities of motivation. She is well aware that her high producers know that she has their interests and futures in mind. She doesn't take them for granted, or for simply what they have to offer while they work for her. And Martha's managers have ample evidence that she has the long-term well-being of the company in mind too.

Following are the kinds of rewards that will serve to recognize good performance and motivate more of the same:

Types of Rewards

- Expanding responsibility on the same level (job enlargement)
- Adding responsibility from above (job enrichment)
- A new or larger territory
- A chance to be account executive on a prestigious account
- Payment for education and higher skills training
- Assignment to a task force or a consulting project
- Freer, quicker, more frequent access to you
- An informal relationship with you

- Acting as adviser or consultant to you
- Coaching by you
- Career coaching by you or some other person
- Public and private praise
- An interview in the company publication
- Liaison with other salespeople or home office personnel
- Bigger base salary
- A financial bonus
- Preferential treatment in scheduling vacations
- Promotion—or the preparation for one
- More desirable equipment or office furnishings
- A better or newer car
- Greater freedom from supervision
- Latitude in making certain decisions (without clearing or checking with you)
- Chairing a meeting for you
- Planning a meeting for salespeople
- Running a meeting for salespeople
- Training another salesperson
- Representing you at a home office meeting
- A business trip in your stead
- Lunch or dinner on the company
- A party or reception in the salesperson's honor
- A gift—plant, book, clothing
- A chance to oversee the territory when you're away
- Assignment as troubleshooter in the territory
- Preferred assignments
- A presentation to home office visitors
- A presentation to higher management
- A private office
- An office with a preferred location
- An assistant
- A sabbatical for self-renewal
- Greater tolerance for occasional time off
- Traveling with you on occasion
- Fact-finding assignments
- A verbal thank you.

No doubt some of the items on this list will stimulate your thinking. You might make a list of rewards that you would appreciate for yourself and see how suitable they are for others.

The better you know your people, the easier it is for you to be creative about the rewards you can provide them. Sometimes the reward possibilities are right in front of your eyes. For example, I conducted a motivation workshop for a group of claims managers for a large insurance company. During the session, I asked them to list the kinds of rewards they had seen managers give, the kinds they themselves had offered their employees, and the kinds they would like to receive from their bosses. They made the lists in small groups, and among the rewards described by two of the groups was the word *door*. In the general discussion that followed, I asked those two groups to explain what they meant. It seems that they worked in cubicles that had no doors and, consequently, there was little privacy. Had their managers said, "How about a door for your office?" they would have been delighted and gratified. It's a good illustration of the small steps that managers can take to tell their subordinates how much they appreciate their efforts. Doors would have cost very little, but the payoff would have been great—and continuing. Every time they opened or closed the door, there would have been a reminder.

A Universal Formula for Getting Change Accepted

You may recall that much earlier in this book I said that you could sell the notion of continuing a change or improvement to your salespeople if you practiced this formula:

- Make it interesting.
- Make it valuable.
- Make it easy.

You'll notice that this formula is closely related to the four R's in adult learning: relevance, realism, resources, rewards (see Chapter 1). You make improvement interesting because it will help your salespeople get more of the results they want more often. You make change valuable to them because that change is the means for them to achieve their personal goals, and because successful improvement efforts lead to more rewards from you. And you make it all easy for them—as easy as possible—through your supervision of the change effort. You provide your salespeople with opportunities for realistic application of new knowledge, techniques, and competencies. And you play a partnership role, bringing the resources you have to bear on their determination and work to become even better in their selling.

A Final Word

Many sales managers confuse inspiration with motivation. A general agent I worked with in a large life insurance company insisted that his agents attend Saturday morning sessions in the office, during which he fervently preached the gospel of success in selling. Some sports figures have launched lucrative second careers by hitting the lecture circuit to tell salespeople how to excel even when the going gets rough. And in my field of training, there are any number of self-made gurus who are willing to share the secrets of the enormous success they have enjoyed. But inspiration is not necessarily motivation. Preaching is quite appropriate in the pulpit, but the most highly motivated salespeople are often very low-key people who tend not to be turned on by apostles of the message, "I've done it. You can do it too." That sort of inspiration is usually momentary.

The mark of true professionals, it seems to me, is an enduring drive to grow, to become more effective, to excel, to literally exhaust their capacities to perform what they have chosen as their work. They may not turn their backs on celebrities, or on the enthusiastic entertainment of sales missionaries. But not for a moment do these successful salespeople confuse an occasional and temporary high with genuine growth and progress. The sales professional says, "I want to be better this month than I was last month. And still better next month." That takes much more than getting fired up. It takes a continuing program that helps the salesperson upgrade selling skills.

Your salespeople rely on you, their manager, to help them actualize their potential. You are there in the trenches with them. You've evaluated their strengths and particular talents. You can point the way to greater effectiveness. And you're available to advise, teach, and counsel. Managers who don't take continual training and development seriously are cheating themselves, their salespeople, and their companies. In many cases, such managers say to themselves, "Look, it's working fine, with an adjustment here, a tune-up there, it will keep on running." That's known as maintenance management, which in this fast-moving world, doesn't really work. The economy doesn't remain static. There will always be new technology. Your competitors are never quite predictable. And the needs of customers change as their businesses and industries evolve. Salespeople have to adapt to the changing environment in which they sell. Otherwise, the process known as entropy sets in. There is decline, stagnation, and even bankruptcy. Salespeople in the latter part of the twentieth century, as never before, must continue to sharpen their skills and competencies.

Other managers live by the familiar slogan, "If it ain't broke, don't fix it." That may be a good operating philosophy for machines, which don't have an innate need to grow and improve themselves. Machines have operational limits, but people don't, necessarily. The vast majority will probably never reach their highest capabilities, but your best salespeople will never stop trying.

Growth and progress, the need to actualize one's potential, provide you with a great motivating force in your salespeople. All you have to do is take advantage of it. Be constantly on the lookout for ways in which your salespeople can improve themselves and upgrade their skills. When you do that, you'll never run out of highly motivated people who want to work for and with you. You'll not only build the level of trust and respect between you, but you'll very likely create a winning sales team, year after year after year.

Index